ore

LIBREX

4

160.

THE LION
Easter Book

WRITTEN AND COMPILED BY MARY BATCHELOR

A LION BOOK

Published by
Lion Publishing plc
Sandy Lane West, Littlemore, Oxford, England
ISBN 0 7459 1573 6

Albatross Books Pty Ltd
PO Box 320, Sutherland, NSW 2232, Australia
ISBN 0 7324 0020 1

First edition 1987

This paperback edition 1989

British Library Cataloguing in Publication Data
Batchelor, Mary
    The Lion Easter book.
    1. Easter
    I. Title
    263'.93   BV55
    ISBN 0-7459-1573-6

Printed and bound in Italy

Acknowledgements
Bible quotations are from *Good News Bible*, copyright 1966,
1971 and 1976 American Bible Society; published by Bible
Societies/Collins. ● Pages 23 and 26: stories retold from *Miracle
on the River Kwai*, by Ernest Gordon, published by Collins.
● Pages 24-25: extract from Michele Guinness, *Child of the
Covenant*, published by Hodder and Stoughton, by permission of
the author and publisher. ● Page 27 (and quotation, page 46):
Oscar Romero story adapted from David Watson and Simon
Jenkins, *Jesus Then and Now*, Lion Publishing. ● Page 31:
Valeri Barinov story from Keston broadsheet, *Right to Believe*,
July 1984; Mark's story from Keston broadsheet, *Right to Believe*,
Spring 1984; retold by permission of Keston College. ● Pages
32-33 and 39: extracts from C. S. Lewis, *The Lion, the Witch and
the Wardrobe*, © by the Estate of C. S. Lewis 1950, published by
Collins and in the USA by Macmillan Publishing Company.
● Page 34: hymn, 'A purple robe' © Timothy Dudley-Smith, by
permission of the author and for USA and Canada by Hope
Publishing Company, Carol Stream, Illinois 60188, USA. ● Page
41: poem, 'Open' © Luci Shaw from *A Widening Light*, by
permission of the author and Harold Shaw Publishers. ● Page
43: extract from *Kilvert's Diary 1870-1879*, ed. William Plomer,
Penguin Books. ● Pages 45 and 54: extract from Michael
Bourdeaux, *Risen Indeed*, published and copyright by Darton,
Longman and Todd Limited, London and St Vladimir's Seminary
Press, 575 Scarsdale Road, Crestwood, New York 10707; Vasili
Ivanovich Kozlov story retold from the same source; both by
permission of the author and publisher. ● Page 47: quotation
from Michael Green, *Man Alive*, by permission of the publisher,
IVP. This book has recently been re-issued under a new title.
● Page 47: Dr Runcie is reported from an item in *The Times*, 7
April 1985. ● Page 54: carol, 'Now the green blade riseth', by
J. M. C. Crum, from *The Oxford Book of Carols*, by permission of
Oxford University Press. Carol, 'Cheer up, friends and
neighbours' (page 42) and 'Easter eggs! Easter eggs!' (page 45)
are from the same source. ● Page 55: the item on the Auca
Indians is based on material in *Searchlight on Bible Words*,
copyright 1972, used by permission of Wycliffe Bible Translators,
Huntington Beach, CA 92647, USA. ● Page 59: extract from
David Watson, *Fear No Evil*, by permission of the publisher,
Hodder and Stoughton.

Illustrations
Clare Barber, pages 26, 30; June Coupland, page 23; Terry
Gabbey, page 50; John Haysom, page 35; Gillian Hurry, pages
10, 14 (bottom), 21, 48-49, 52; Caroline McDonald-Paul, pages
12, 22, 38 (top), 58; Eira Reeves, pages 13, 20, 25, 53; Helen
Senior, pages 8, 34; Kate Shannon, pages 44, 56; Pamela
Stephens, pages 28, 54; Alison Winfield, pages 16, 33, 38
(bottom); Paul Wrigley, pages 14 (top), 42-43.

Photographs
Andes Press Agency/Carlos Reyes, page 27; Robin Bath, title
page; Michael Cole, page 56; Keith Ellis, page 15; Mary Evans
Picture Library, page 37; Sonia Halliday Photographs/Jane
Taylor, page 17; ITC Entertainment Ltd, pages 29, 30; Lion
Publishing/David Alexander, page 41; Jean-Luc Ray, page 44;
Mick Rock/Cephas Picture Library, page 19; John Rylands
University Library, page 47; John Span, page 58; Tiofoto AB,
page 53; David Townsend, endpapers; D. C. Williamson, page 12;
ZEFA (UK), cover, pages 9, 11, 24, 45, 48, 55, 60.

CONTENTS

CELEBRATING EASTER

Long ago, before the time when the history books begin, each year people used to celebrate the return of spring to the earth. As the trees burst into leaf and the birds began to sing, it seemed to them that the darkness and death of winter had been defeated.

We still observe some of the customs that go back to that earlier age. But for the past two thousand years, Christians have kept a new kind of spring festival. For them, Easter is the most important celebration in the whole year because it was at Eastertime that Jesus died 'for the sins of the whole world' and rose to life again and is alive for ever. On the first Good Friday and Easter Sunday he won the war against darkness and death, once and for all.

For many centuries before Jesus' birth, the Jewish people had their own special spring festival, called Passover. Passover commemorates the time when God rescued the people of Israel from slavery and Moses led them out of Egypt.

Jesus was crucified during Passover time and the first Christians, who were all Jews, turned Passover into the even greater celebration of God's deliverance through Jesus. Jews today who are also Christians, still enjoy a wonderful double celebration of Passover and Easter.

Of course, Easter and springtime do not always go together. In the southern hemisphere, Easter falls in autumn, at the beginning of winter. But because of Jesus' resurrection, it is still a time of new life and new beginnings.

THE NAME FOR EASTER

In many European languages, the name for Easter comes from the word Passover, as the list below will show:

Denmark : *Paaske*
France : *Pâcques*
Holland : *Pasen*
Italy : *Pasqua*
Spain : *Pascua*
Sweden : *Påsk*
Wales : *Pasg*

FIXING THE DATE

Jewish Passover is always celebrated at full moon, so the date and day of the week varies from year to year. Since Jesus rose from death on a Sunday, many early Christians kept Easter Day on the Sunday nearest to Passover. But Jewish Christians preferred to remember Jesus' death on Good Friday on the actual Passover Day, whether or not that was a Friday. So, instead of an Easter weekend, Easter might fall at any time during the week.

That was not the only difference of opinion. There are many ways of calculating the date of Passover — and thus of Easter — which are too complicated for me to understand or explain! Learned scholars made calculations and came up with different answers. People argued hotly about the real date for Easter.

So in the fourth century it was decided to hold a church council at Nicaea to thrash out the whole matter. There they agreed on a method of calculating the date and also decided that Easter Day should always be on a Sunday. But not every part of the church followed those rules.

The Celtic church, for example, had its own way of dating Easter and where the Celtic and Roman churches existed alongside, as in England, things became confusing. In the seventh century, Queen Eanfleda, who had been converted in the south of England by missionaries from Rome, was holding a solemn fast for Palm Sunday, at the same time as her husband, the king of Northumbria, was enjoying his Easter day feast in another part of the palace!

A church synod was held in the beautiful cliff-edge monastery at Whitby, where Hilda was abbess. After speakers from both sides had put their case, the king decided in favour of the Roman reckoning, which the Western church observes to this day. In the Eastern church, a different kind of reckoning is still used, so Easter often falls at a different date. But these days nobody minds!

CALCULATING EASTER DATES

According to the decision of the Council of Nicaea, Easter Day falls on the Sunday following the first full moon after the spring equinox (21 March). In practice, this means that Easter Day can never be earlier than 22 March and never later than 25 April.

In some countries Easter eggs are hidden for the children to find on Easter Day. Here the whole family joins in the fun.

FEASTING AND FASTING

When Jesus was thirty years old, he left the carpenter's shop in Nazareth. But before he began to preach and teach through all the land, he went away by himself into the desert to be alone with God. For forty days, with only the wild beasts for company, he discovered God's purpose for his life. He resisted the temptation to become a popular and successful figure, and faced up to a life of hardship that would end in certain death.

Remembering those weeks, the Christian church set aside the forty days before Easter as a time to practise self-denial and to think and pray quietly to God. That time is called Lent, the word for springtime.

In the Middle Ages, everyone fasted during Lent. That meant going without all the nice things like meat and butter, eggs and cream, and eating only plain fare. Not many people fast as strictly as that these days, but some go without a few of the things they like best during Lent.

Self-denial will not make us good or persuade God to be pleased with us. Easter reminds us that we can never make ourselves good enough for God. Jesus died to do that. But going without sweets or chocolates may be worthwhile if it reminds us not to be selfish and give in to ourselves too often. It is especially good if, in addition, we give the money we have saved to help others.

Some churches hold Lent lunches of bread and cheese and give the money that a full meal for everyone would cost, to feed the hungry of the world. Relief organizations such as Christian Aid and TEAR Fund may suggest other ways of giving to help others during Lent.

WHEN THE CUPBOARD WAS BARE

In the Middle Ages, most people followed a pattern of feasting followed by fasting. There was no cold storage or quick transport to make a steady supply of food possible all year round. So, although there was plenty to eat after a good harvest, once winter was past the stocks had dwindled and Lent would be a lean time, whether the church said so or not!

Today some of us have plenty to eat the whole year, while others are always hungry. Lent is a good time to share the plenty we have with others who have very little, or are starving. But we don't have to wait for Lent to do that! So Lent can be a time for giving — not just giving something up. Some Christians give time and help to others specially during Lent, as well as giving money. There are sure to be those in our road or school or town, as well as on the other side of the world, who need our help.

SHROVE TUESDAY

Shrove Tuesday is the last day before Lent, which begins on Ash Wednesday. In the Middle Ages a church bell used to ring to call everyone to church to be 'shriven' — which means to be given absolution for the sins they confessed.

Shrove Tuesday is called Mardi Gras — or Fat Tuesday — in Europe and South America and parts of the USA. The fast might begin tomorrow, but for this one last day everyone had as much fun as they could.

Pancakes were made from

the butter and cream and eggs that would be forbidden during the next six weeks of Lent. Everyone feasted and made merry. In England, the bell that had solemnly summoned the parish to church to be shriven, later came to be known as the pancake bell. It reminded everyone that the holiday had begun. They could down tools, make their pancakes, and take to the streets for fun and games.

In some countries in Europe there are great carnival processions and all kinds of local fun and games still go on. Strange and wild games of football are played in some places and in others there is a pancake race. One of the best known in England is held at Olney in Buckinghamshire, where housewives race from town square to church, clutching a pan with a pancake in it. Each runner must toss her pancake three times along the route. The winner is the first to arrive at the church with her pancake in one piece.

ASH WEDNESDAY

On Ash Wednesday, first day of Lent, law-breakers and wrongdoers in the town used to have to walk barefoot to church, to show how sorry they were for their sins. Ashes would be put on their foreheads as a sign of repentance. Gradually the friends who came with them, and everyone else too, joined

Mardi Gras (Shrove Tuesday) celebrations in the USA.

in the service of penitence. Roman Catholic churches still keep the custom of Ash Wednesday, and other churches have special services on that day too.

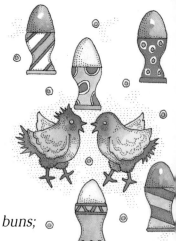

SPECIAL FOOD AT EASTER

> **"** *One a penny, two a penny, hot cross buns;*
> *If your daughters do not like them,*
> *give them to your sons.* **"**
> *TRADITIONAL SONG, 1797*

Like all good festivals, Easter has its own share of special foods. Hot cross buns, eaten on Good Friday, are still popular in Europe and the USA. These spiced currant buns are marked with a paste cross before being baked.

In bygone centuries, people used to believe that hot cross buns had special magical powers, provided that they were baked on Good Friday. So bakers and housewives got up very early to make them on the actual day.

Perhaps such buns were made long ago, when the cross was a pagan sign. But Christians remember Jesus' death on a cross on the first Good Friday.

In the old days, some of the batch of buns would be purposely left in the oven to harden, so that they would keep for a whole year. Then, during winter, part of a bun would be grated into medicine as a cure for sickness. Sailors going to sea would take a hot cross bun with them to guard against shipwreck!

Easter day is also associated with special food. Boiled eggs are often served at breakfast, when Easter cards and gifts may be exchanged. Roast lamb, which is the main dish at Jewish Passover, is served at the main meal in many places.

In Poland, the food is set out ready all day long, so that everyone can eat just when they feel like it. The table is decorated with green leaves and a sugar lamb may be placed as a centre-piece.

There is always a fine feast of cold meats and salads and plenty of eggs. Children take samples of food to church to be blessed by the priest, since he no longer has time to visit every home to say a blessing as he once did.

In Britain, traditionally simnel cake is baked for tea and bakers still export simnel cakes to descendants of early English settlers in the USA. Originally the simnel cake was a gift to mothers on

Poland has its own special Easter food.

Mothering Sunday in mid-Lent and there is a record of simnel cakes in church annals as far back as 1072. No one is quite sure what the word simnel means, though most agree that it comes from the Latin *simila*, which means fine flour.

Some tell the story that simnel is the combined names of a married couple, Simon and Nell, who had a disagreement about how to cook their fruit cake. One wanted to boil it, the other to bake it. In the end they used both methods and the cake is named after both of them.

These days a simnel cake is baked with a layer of marzipan in the middle of the fruit mixture. It is decorated with marzipan too, with eleven marzipan balls to represent the twelve apostles, minus Judas.

PANCAKE SPECIAL

Pancakes are fun to make and eat all through the year, but they are specially associated with the days before Lent. They taste good with sweet or savoury fillings. In the USSR during Shrovetide, which they call *Myas lanitza* (butter week), they eat pancakes called *blini*, made with yeast. They are served with melted butter and sour cream.

A seventeenth-century recipe for 'fine pancakes' begins:

'Take a pint of cream and six new-laid eggs, beat them very well together, put in a quarter of a pound of sugar and one nutmeg or a little beaten mace (which you please) and so much flour as will thicken . . . Your pan must be heated reasonable hot and wiped with a clean cloth, this done put in your batter as thick or thin as you please.'

Here is a recipe for plainer pancakes, which you can try. (Always take great care when using hot fat and a hot pan. Make sure that an adult knows what you are doing and is on hand if needed.)

To make 12 pancakes you will need:
100g plain flour/1 cup all-purpose flour
2 eggs
300ml/1 ¾ cups milk
pinch of salt
1 tablespoon of oil
white vegetable fat

1 Sieve the flour and salt into a basin and make a little well in the middle.

2 Pour the eggs into the hollow and gradually add half the milk, mixing with a wooden spoon to get rid of lumps. Beat until it is quite smooth, then mix in the rest of the milk. Just before you are ready to cook the pancakes, stir in the oil.

3 Melt a very little vegetable fat in a frying-pan until it is very hot (use only enough fat each time to grease the pan). Put about two tablespoons of batter into the pan and tip the pan a little, to spread the batter all over the bottom of the pan.

4 Cook at medium heat until the underside is brown, then toss the pancake over and cook the other side. (Make sure that you catch it in the pan!)

5 Keep cooked pancakes warm by stacking them between two plates over a pan of simmering water. This way they won't get dried out.

6 Serve them with lemon juice and sugar or honey or maple syrup, or roll them up around any filling you like to invent.

A DAY FOR MOTHERS

In America, Australia and many other countries, Mother's Day is kept on the second Sunday in May. It was Miss Anna Jarvis of Philadelphia who in 1907 suggested that one day a year should be set aside for mothers. She arranged a special church service and asked everyone who came to wear a white carnation in honor of their mother. The custom caught on and spread.

In Britain, Mothering Sunday falls on the middle Sunday of Lent and in days gone by it was a time when the strict Lenten fast could be broken. Everyone in England used to walk to the parish church, which was the 'mother' church, instead of attending a nearby chapel of ease, as they usually did.

Mothering Sunday soon became a family day, too, when sons and daughters who had left home to serve apprenticeships, or go to work in a big house, would come back to the family for the day.

Sometimes a girl would bring her mother a special cake that she or her mistress had baked and both boys and girls would pick bunches of violets for their mothers, as they walked home through the woods. When the whole family had been to church, they would have a special dinner and enjoy the rest of the holiday together.

Since the Second World

CARDS TO MAKE

Mothers usually prefer a card that you have made yourself to one you have bought in the shop. You can draw any picture you like on the front. If you paint a house, you can make a door that opens to show the family inside.

Flowers are a usual Mothers' Day gift, and a card with flowers on is another idea. If you can't draw or paint well, cut out flowers from a nurseryman's catalogue or a magazine and stick them on the front. Draw a bowl or container for them.

Inside the card put a verse or message for your mother that you have made up yourself.

Flowers for mother are a special feature of Mothering Sunday and of Mothers' Day.

War, Mothering Sunday has more often been known as Mothers' Day. Perhaps some of the US soldiers and airmen stationed in Britain brought over their own customs.

Whatever the date, it is good to have one special day when we can thank our mothers and make a special fuss of them.

A HELPING HAND

Perhaps the biggest treat for mothers is to be free from all the usual chores for one day. You may decide to take her breakfast in bed, or to wash all the dishes and prepare the vegetables for dinner. If there is more than one of you in the family, you can work out a scheme beforehand for sharing out the jobs. The greatest treat of all for mothers is to hear the children working happily together, without fighting or complaining!

HOUSEHOLD CHECK-LIST

if you are not clever at making things, here is an idea for a very useful gift.

First make a thorough search of the kitchen, looking in cupboards and on shelves. Make a note of all the foods, cleaning materials and other items that are used in your home. (Don't forget such things as light bulbs and cooking foil.)

Then arrange all the items on your list in alphabetical order. You may like to divide them under separate headings too, such as: Canned foods, Preserves and Pickles, and so on. Copy out your list very neatly onto a large piece of card. You can colour a border to make it look pretty. Whenever your mother goes shopping, she will be able to use your check-list to remind her of the items she may need to buy.

HERE COMES THE KING!

The people of the Hebrews
With palms before thee went;
Our praise and prayer and anthems
Before thee we present!
THEODULF OF ORLEANS, 750-821

In spring time, hundreds of Jewish families began the journey to Jerusalem, their capital city, to celebrate the festival of Passover.

Jesus and his disciples set off for Jerusalem too, and were soon joined by other groups of pilgrims along the route.

Before they arrived, Jesus sent two of his disciples to fetch a young donkey, so that he could ride into the city.

Some of them made a saddle from their cloaks, and Jesus climbed on the donkey's back. The donkey had never been ridden before, but it was not frightened, even though the crowds jostled and shouted.

As Jesus began the steep ride, the boys and girls ran alongside, shouting and cheering. Some people hurried ahead, so that they could lay their cloaks down in the road. Others cut down branches from nearby trees to line the path. It was a route fit for a king.

Pilgrims who were already in Jerusalem heard that Jesus was on his way. They streamed out of the city to meet him, waving palm branches in welcome.

'Praise God!' they all shouted. 'Praise to King David's son! God bless the one who comes in God's name!'

THE PROMISED KING

There was a special reason why the crowds were so excited when Jesus rode the donkey into Jerusalem. Long before, God had promised through the prophets that he would send the Messiah, his anointed King, to save and rule his people Israel. He would be descended from their great King David.

For three years people had watched and listened to Jesus and many had recognized him as that promised King.

When they saw him riding into Jerusalem at the head of a procession, they hoped he was coming to be crowned in Jerusalem. Soon he would lead an army against the hated Roman rulers, whose soldiers tramped their streets. He would set their country free!

But Jesus had not chosen to be that kind of king. He chose to rule by love, not force. He was not going to show his might by fighting a foreign army but by dying like a criminal on a Roman cross.

When he rode on a donkey he wanted the crowds to remember the words that the prophet Zechariah had written, hundreds of years before:

'Rejoice, people of Zion! Shout for joy, you people of Jerusalem! Look, your king is coming to you! He comes triumphant and victorious, but humble and riding on a donkey.'

A king who went to battle rode a horse. A king who came in peace rode a donkey. Jesus had come to bring peace to every single person who owns him king.

PALM SUNDAY

The Sunday before Easter is called Palm Sunday because the crowds waved palm branches as they followed Jesus' procession into Jerusalem. From early Christian days, churches have been decorated with palm on this Sunday. In countries too cold for palm to grow, willow catkins are often used instead. Sometimes every one who comes to the Palm Sunday service is given a little cross made of palm.

DONKEYS

During the Middle Ages a Palm Sunday carnival was held in some countries, led by the bishop riding a real donkey. In later years a carved wooden donkey was carried instead. These wooden donkeys were called palmesels.

At the time of the Reformation, in the sixteenth century, Palm Sunday carnivals were banned in Protestant countries and one palmesel was thrown into the river at Zurich! But others have survived and may still be seen in museums in Germany and Switzerland.

If you look at any donkey's back, you will see a brown patch in the shape of a cross. Legend says that every donkey has carried the sign of the cross since the day the donkey carried Jesus into Jerusalem, so soon before his crucifixion.

MY KING!

Christians obey and worship Jesus as King. Sometimes their loyalty costs them their lives. In the early days of the church, Christians were faced with a terrible choice. Under Roman rule, every citizen was ordered to take an oath of allegiance to the Roman emperor, Caesar, owning him as lord and god. Many Christians refused to do so and were thrown to the lions, or burned at the stake.

In 156 an excited mob shouted for Polycarp, Bishop of Smyrna, to be brought before officials to take the oath. He refused, but the Roman official did his best to save such an old man from so cruel a death.

'What harm can there be in saying that Caesar is lord?' he asked him. 'You have only to do that and to speak out against Christ, and your life will be spared.'

But Polycarp answered, 'Eighty-six years have I served him, and he has done me no wrong. How then can I speak evil of my King, who saved me?'

Reluctantly the official gave orders and Polycarp was burned at the stake.

The Palm Sunday procession in Jerusalem moves down from the Mount of Olives towards the old city and temple area.

THE SHADOWS LENGTHEN

“ *Jesus said:*
As long as it is day, we must keep on doing the
work of him who sent me; night is coming
when no one can work. While I am in the
world, I am the light for the world. ”
From JOHN'S GOSPEL, CHAPTER 9

DAYTIME

During Passover week, Jesus and his disciples stayed with their friends, Martha, Mary and Lazarus, at Bethany. Every day they walked the short distance into Jerusalem, where Jesus taught the crowds in the temple courts.

Martha and Mary loved Jesus dearly and were so thankful to him for bringing their brother, Lazarus, back from death.

One evening they planned a special supper party. Martha was busy all day, cooking tasty dishes. Even when everyone else was at the table, she was still going backwards and forwards, bringing in more food and wine.

Jesus looked around at all his friends, glad to have them close. But Mary was so full of love and thankfulness to Jesus that she wanted to show him how she felt. She slipped quietly away and came back carrying her most treasured possession — a delicate flask of very costly perfume. Moving silently to Jesus' place at the table, she poured all the contents of the bottle over his feet, quickly wiping the drops with her long hair. The scent began to fill the whole house.

Jesus understood how Mary felt and why she had done such a thing. He connected it with what was soon to happen. At that time, when a person died, those who loved him would anoint his body with perfume and spices before burying it.

But it was Judas Iscariot's voice that broke the silence.

'What a waste!' he exclaimed harshly. 'She's squandered all that expensive perfume! We could have sold it at top price and given the proceeds to the poor.'

Jesus spoke up quickly.

'Don't say anything against Mary!' he said. 'You will always be able to help the poor. But I shall not be with you for long. Mary has done something special and beautiful. She has prepared my body for the burial which is soon to come. What she has done will never be forgotten.'

THE COMING NIGHT

While Jesus was with his friends at Bethany, his enemies were busy in the darkness, plotting against him. Already they had made it known that anyone who was able to give information leading to Jesus' arrest should get in touch with them.

'We will meet at my house,' Caiaphas, the leading priest, told the other conspirators. 'We have got to find a way to arrest Jesus and have him executed as soon as possible.'

But although they desperately wanted to get rid of Jesus, they were afraid to make any move against him during the Passover Festival. There were too many in the excitable crowds who loved him and might start a riot if they saw him arrested.

Shadows lengthen as the sun goes down and night approaches.

'If only we knew where we could find him on his own,' they said. 'Then we could arrest him and have him tried and sentenced to death before anyone has time to demonstrate.'

TRAITOR IN THE CAMP

It was not only Jesus' enemies who wanted to put an end to Jesus' life. Judas Iscariot, one of Jesus' twelve close disciples, was growing more and more discontented. He had hoped from the beginning that Jesus would soon make himself king and drive out the hated Roman army of occupation.

But the more he came to know Jesus, the more he began to realize that this dream would never come true. That evening at Bethany, Jesus had talked about his own death and burial. It seemed that he was not even prepared to fight to save his own skin.

Judas had had enough. He slipped away from the supper party and strode along the dark roads until he came to the Jerusalem mansion of Caiaphas.

'How much will you pay me if I help you to find Jesus?' he asked the conspirators.

'Thirty silver pieces,' they replied at once, and one of them counted out the shining silver coins into his outstretched hand, before he could change his mind.

'Give me a little time,' Judas said. 'I'll let you know as soon as I can where you will be able to find him unprotected and away from the crowds.'

FRIENDS OR DESERTERS?

Jesus went on warning his disciples that he would soon be taken prisoner and handed over to the Roman officials to be sentenced to death. They could not believe their ears. But whatever might happen, they were sure that they would stand by their leader.

'I'll stick by you if you're taken to prison — or even if you die!' Peter exclaimed. 'I'll never leave you, whatever the others may do!'

'We won't leave you either!' the rest insisted indignantly.

Jesus shook his head sadly. 'You will all run away and leave me when the time comes,' he told them. 'You, Peter, will say three times over that you do not even know me.'

But that dark and bitter night had not yet come.

PREPARING FOR EASTER

Preparations begin long in advance for every special occasion. Getting ready for Easter is just as important as getting ready for Christmas.

The weeks of Lent were once the time when new Christians, who were to be baptized on Easter Eve, were taught about the Christian faith and life. Those who had already been baptized thought again about the promises they had once made and promised to be true to them.

Everyone was preparing for the special Easter Communion. Wrongs were confessed and quarrels made up. Lent was the time for

EASTER CARDS TO MAKE

When you make your own Easter cards, remember that the best ones remind us of the real meaning of Easter. Of course, Easter eggs and chicks, and flowers too, tell us about new life and new beginnings, which are an important part of the Easter story. Here is one idea.

The Empty Tomb

Fold a piece of thin card in half. (If you have no card, fold a large piece of paper — 29×21cms — in half and glue it together. Then fold again to make your card.)

Near the top of the card, draw the outline of a hill, in green or brown, and put three crosses on top.

Near the bottom of the picture draw a rough circle to represent the stone that covered Jesus' tomb. All round you can draw trees and flowers, because the tomb was in a garden.

Cut carefully round the circle, leaving an uncut hinge on the left side. The stone can then be lifted away to show what is inside.

In the empty tomb you can write the angel's words: 'He is not here, he is risen!' or just put, 'Jesus is alive today!' Then add your own Easter message.

Gift Card

Your Easter card can be a gift, too. Paint a picture on the front of the card: then buy a packet of seeds and staple it to the inside. Choose from vegetable, flower, or herb seeds — whichever the person you are giving to would like best.

If the seeds are for a young brother or sister, read the instructions on the packet, to make sure that they are easy to grow.

Seeds make a good Easter gift because they are an example of dying and coming to life in a new and better way, as Jesus did.

Inside the card you could write the Bible words, 'Christ died for our sins, was buried and raised to life three days later.'

spring-cleaning lives, as well as homes.

Many churches today hold special Lent services. In some towns the churches of different denominations join together in groups to discuss and share their Christian faith. During Holy Week — the week in which Good Friday falls — drama groups may act out the events of the last days in Jesus' life, inside church or, more often, out in the open air.

In some churches you will discover a little 'tomb' carved out of the stone wall and decorated with carvings to depict the Easter story. Sometimes, on Easter Day, the clergy act out the visit to the tomb of Peter and John and the women. In other churches a model of the scene at the tomb on that first Easter morning is made and decorated with flowers.

Perhaps you can think of ways in which you can get ready for Easter in your family as well as at school.

A PRESENT TO MAKE
Woolly Chick

If there is a baby in the family, or neighbourhood, a woolly chicken makes a good present. You will need to make two woollen balls out of yellow wool, one for the body and a smaller one for the head.

To make a woollen ball

1 Make two circles of cardboard about 8cms in diameter and cut out a smaller circle inside each about 2.5cms diameter.

2 Wind the wool around both rings, from inside the holes, until the holes are too small for any more wool to go through. (It may help to thread through with a darning needle towards the end.)

3 Cut the wool around the outside edge, between the two rings.

4 Tie a strong piece of thread between the rings and fasten it tightly. Now you can safely take out the cardboard and fluff out the ball.

5 Make a smaller ball in the same way and sew the two together to make the chick. You can also sew on black feet and eyes and an orange beak if you wish. *Never* use beads or buttons which could come off and be dangerous to a baby.

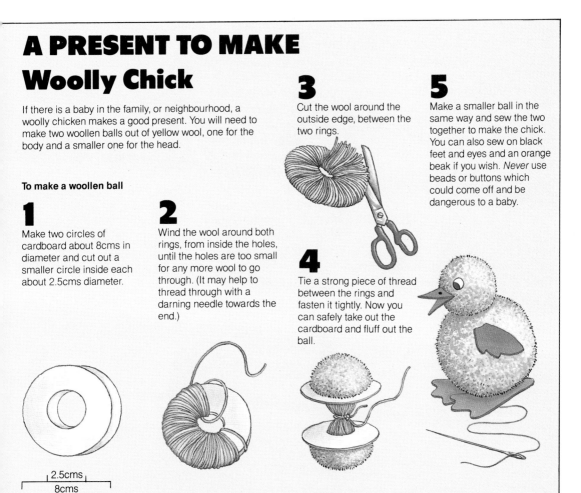

2.5cms
8cms

LOOKING AFTER OTHERS

On the Sunday before Good Friday, Jesus rode into Jerusalem on a donkey, cheered by the crowds.

On the Thursday he sat down to supper with his twelve close friends, knowing that it would be the last meal they would have together before he died. Later that night his enemies would arrest him.

But as Jesus looked around the table his mind was full of his friends and not of himself. He loved them all very much, even Judas Iscariot, who was planning to betray him to his enemies.

In those days, before guests sat down to eat a slave would wash their travel-stained feet. But there was no slave here. A pitcher of water and a towel lay ready, but not one of the disciples was willing to do such a dirty and despised job for the others. So they went on talking, their sandalled feet still hot and dusty from their journey.

Then Jesus got up, poured some water into a bowl, and tied the towel loosely around his waist. Then he went from one disciple to the next, washing their feet and drying them gently with the towel.

They all felt very ashamed that Jesus, their leader, should be left to do such a job for them and Peter tried to stop him.

Jesus explained that anyone who wanted to belong to him must let him make them pure and clean. Washing their feet was a picture of the way in which he would make them new, 'clean' people by dying for their sins.

When Jesus had finished he sat down again and talked to them.

'You call me your Master and Lord,' he said, 'and you are right to do so. But although I am your master, I was willing to wait on you as a slave because I love you so much. You must follow my example and look after one another's needs. Don't be full of your own importance and your own concerns. If you obey me and copy me, you will be really happy.'

MAUNDY THURSDAY

The day on which Jesus washed his disciples' feet is called Maundy Thursday. Some think that the name is taken from the Latin word *mandatum*, which means 'command', because Jesus commanded his followers to love and serve one another.

From early times there have been special ceremonies on Maundy Thursday, when Jesus' action has been literally copied.

Each Maundy Thursday the Pope still washes the feet of twelve priests.

In England the sovereign used to wash the feet of as many old people as the years he had lived. King James II was the last to do this, in 1685.

Nowadays in England Queen Elizabeth II attends a Maundy Day service in Westminster Abbey, or some other cathedral, and distributes special coins — Maundy money — to one man and one woman for every year of her age.

There are many ways of obeying Jesus' command without having to wash someone's feet! Some young people, for example, give up their own holiday to go away with groups who are elderly or disabled. They take care of them in every way so that they can enjoy a holiday they could never otherwise have.

Love in Action on the River Kwai

During the Second World War, Japanese prisoner of war camps were places of death and despair. The prisoners were forced to work until they dropped, building bridges or working to construct the railroad to Burma. Many fell ill from exhaustion, disease, or lack of food, and many died.

Captain Ernest Gordon was among the prisoners of war who were marched into the jungle to build a bridge over the River Kwai. He became desperately ill, suffering, among other things, from dysentery, malaria and diphtheria and its after effects. He could not bear the stench and airlessness of the sleeping platform reserved for sick prisoners, and he asked to be moved to a place in the open air, where the bodies of those who died were stacked.

One day he heard the doctors say that he would soon die. But prisoner friends built him a little hut and furnished it with a bed of split bamboo, covered with clean rice sacks. Gently and carefully they carried his thin body and laid it on the bed. Then two fellow prisoners came to see him, offering to nurse him. He was too ill to do anything for himself.

Both men were Christians. Dusty was a Methodist and Dinty a Roman Catholic. Dusty set to work at once. He fetched warm water and some rags and gave Captain Gordon the first wash he had enjoyed for weeks. Then, with great care and gentleness, he cleaned the sores and ulcers that covered his legs. Before he left he sprinkled the dirt floor of the hut with water and swept it clean.

In the evening, when Dusty had to report for duty in the kitchen, Dinty, who had finished work for the day, took over as night nurse.

First thing in the morning, Dusty reappeared with a breakfast of rice. Then he would set about washing the Captain and tending his ulcers. Next he began to massage the wasted limbs to bring back some feeling and strengthen the muscles.

Gordon began to get better.

In time he took his first few stumbling steps. His own courage and determination completed the recovery.

The love and care of those two Christians had saved him from certain death, but neither had said much about their faith, until asked. Both clearly showed Jesus' love in their willingness to do even the most unpleasant tasks cheerfully and kindly.

Captain Gordon and some of the other prisoners began to read about Jesus in the Gospels and let his love come into their own lives. Soon they wanted to show his love to others.

The whole camp was transformed.

Before, everyone had fought for his own rights. Now, men thought of one another's needs. Selfishness and despair shrivelled up and happiness and hope grew strong as more and more prisoners began to share the love and care of Jesus, for his sake.

THE LAST MEAL TOGETHER

Blessed art thou, O Lord our God, King of the universe, who hast kept us alive, sustained us, and brought us to enjoy this festive season.
From THE JEWISH HAGGADAH (service book for Passover)

PASSOVER

Long ago, when the Jewish people were slaves in Egypt, God sent Moses to set them free and bring them through the desert to the promised land — a country of their own.

The night before they left, the angel of death struck every home in Egypt. God's people, having obeyed his instructions, were safe inside their homes. They ate the first Passover Feast of roast lamb, their baggage ready packed for the journey that would soon begin. Later, Moses instructed them to keep an annual festival to commemorate God's wonderful rescue operation.

The main Passover dish is still roast lamb. Unleavened bread — flat biscuits made without yeast — remind the Jewish people that their ancestors were in such a hurry that there was no time for the dough to be left to rise before they set out.

A bowl of salt water and another of bitter-tasting herbs remind them of the tears they shed, and the unhappiness they endured, during their years as slaves.

Four different cups of wine are served, standing for God's four promises to his people, which you can find in the Bible, in Exodus chapter 6, verses 6-7.

At every Passover Feast, the youngest in the family asks what the celebration means, and the head of the family gives the answers.

The blessing of the wine is an important moment in the Passover celebration.

A CHILD'S PASSOVER

Michele Guinness was brought up in a Jewish family in the north-east of England. Now that she is also a Christian, she keeps both Jewish Passover and Christian Easter with her own children.

In her book, *Child of the Covenant*, she recalls Passover in her home about twenty years ago. Her young brother David used to ask the questions and her uncle, Mark, who led the service, gave the answers.

'We made our way to the

table, and what a table it was! The cloth was bleached until it dazzled and crinkled when you moved up against it. The best silver had been polished until you could see your own reflection quite clearly. Each person had a tiny silver wine goblet, which shimmered in the candle-light. An embroidered coverlet, draped over three pieces of unleavened bread, added a startling dash of scarlet and sapphire. David and I took our places, wide-eyed and open-mouthed . . . We opened our *Haggadahs*, the appropriate opening blessings were made, Gran lit the candles, then David read out the famous four questions:

' "Why is this night different from all other nights and why do we eat unleavened bread?"

' "Why do we eat bitter herbs instead of vegetables?"

' "Why do we dip in the dish twice?"

' "Why do we eat leaning?"

' "And why do you ask the same questions every year?" grinned Mark, "because you always get the same answer." '

THE LAST SUPPER

Jesus said to his disciples: 'I have wanted so much to eat this Passover meal with you before I suffer! For I tell you, I will never eat it until it is given its full meaning in the Kingdom of God.'
From LUKE'S GOSPEL, CHAPTER 22

While Jesus and his friends were sharing the Passover meal, Jesus transformed the ceremony into something new, which Christians have celebrated every since.

Moses had made a firm agreement between God and the people of Israel, solemnly sealing it with animals' blood. Jesus was soon to give his life blood, so that God could make a new agreement, or covenant, with all people everywhere who put their trust in him.

Here are Jesus' own words that night:

'While they were eating, Jesus took a piece of bread, gave a prayer of thanks, broke it, and gave it to his disciples. "Take and eat it," he said; "this is my body."

'Then he took a cup, gave thanks to God, and gave it to them. "Drink it, all of you," he said; "this is my blood, which seals God's covenant, my blood poured out for many for the forgiveness of sins." '
From MATTHEW'S GOSPEL, CHAPTER 26

From the very beginning, Christians obeyed Jesus' instructions and celebrated 'The Lord's Supper' when they met together. Nearly all Christian churches do so still, some daily, some weekly, some monthly or even less often.

Different names are used for this important Christian celebration. Here are some of them:

Holy Communion — Communion means sharing. St Paul writes about sharing the body and blood of Christ.

Eucharist — Eucharist means thanksgiving.

Mass — Probably from the Latin *missa*, used at the end of the service.

The Sacrament — An abbreviation of The Sacrament of the Lord's Supper. Sacrament means something sacred or holy.

The Lord's Supper/The Breaking of Bread — Both used in the New Testament for the meal shared by Christians which included this celebration.

COCONUT PYRAMIDS

At Passover it is also traditional to eat sweet things, symbolizing the promised land. Michele Guinness has sent this recipe for coconut pyramids specially for our book, for you to make and enjoy.

You will need:
2 eggs
200g/8oz dried coconut
100g/4oz sugar
the rind and juice of half a
*   lemon*

1
Beat the eggs and sugar until creamy, then add grated lemon rind, lemon juice and coconut.

2
Form the pyramids by pressing small amounts of the mixture into a moist eggcup.

3
Bake the pyramids for 15-20 minutes until brown: Gas 5/ 373°F/190°C. This quantity makes 24 pyramids.

THE DARKNESS DEEPENS

Jesus said, 'While I am in the world, I am the light of the world.'

St John said, 'The light has come into the world, but men love the darkness rather than the light, because their deeds are evil.'
From JOHN'S GOSPEL, CHAPTERS 9 and 3

Many ordinary people loved Jesus for his goodness and absolute truth as well as for his kindness and love. But many of the religious leaders hated him. He saw through their pretended piety and was not afraid to say so. His perfect goodness showed up their own wrongdoing, just as the whiteness of snow makes everything else look dirty.

These leaders wanted to keep power in their own hands and they were jealous of Jesus' popularity too. But now that Judas, one of his own men, had agreed to inform on Jesus, they hoped soon to arrest him and get rid of him for ever.

When Jesus sat down to the last supper with his friends, Judas was there. Although he had not breathed a word about his betrayal to anyone, Jesus knew about it.

During the meal he said, 'One of you is going to give me away to my enemies.'

The disciples were horrified.

'It isn't me, Lord, is it?' they asked him, one after another.

'The traitor is here, sharing the meal,' Jesus said. Once more he showed his love and forgiveness for Judas by helping him to the choicest bit of food. But Judas' face was set and grim.

Jesus looked at him and said, 'Be quick about what you are going to do.'

The others guessed nothing. Judas was in charge of funds and they thought that Jesus was telling him to hurry to the shops.

Judas gave no answer. He left the friendly light of the lamps and the warmth of the meal table, and went out into the darkness of the night. He walked swiftly towards the place where he would find his new masters. Now he could tell them what they wanted to hear. He knew that, when supper was over, Jesus would go with the disciples to a peaceful olive-orchard, where they often walked and talked quietly together. No one but

their friend, the owner of the garden, would know they were there. It was the ideal place in which to find and arrest Jesus.

IN THE MASTER'S FOOTSTEPS

Jesus said to his friends, 'If the world hates you, just remember that it hated me first.'
From JOHN'S GOSPEL, CHAPTER 15

All down the ages, good people have been abused and hounded to death by bad people. No race or country has been free from guilt. But when Jesus' followers suffer for doing right, they find comfort in knowing that they are walking in the footsteps of their Master.

DUSTY MILLER

In *Looking After Others* (page 23) the story is told of Captain Gordon, a prisoner of war during the Second World War, who was nursed back to health through the loving care of a Christian called Dusty Miller.

Later the two were in different camps and lost touch. When the war was ending, Gordon eagerly asked the couriers who went from camp to camp distributing food, what had happened to Dusty.

At last he found one who knew, but at first he would not reply. Then he admitted that Dusty had been in trouble for making a Japanese officer angry.

'What had he done wrong?' Gordon asked.

'That was it,' the courier explained, 'he hadn't done anything wrong. The officer hated him just because he was good. Whatever he did to him, Dusty would never react in anger or violence.'

Gordon asked how it had all ended.

'They strung him up to a tree,' the courier replied briefly.

'You mean that they crucified him?' Gordon asked, aghast.

'Yes, they crucified him.'

OSCAR ROMERO

The right-wing military government of El Salvador supported Oscar Romero as the new archbishop of San Salvador in 1977 because they thought that he was too gentle and shy to give them any trouble. He would be a puppet leader of the church. But only a few weeks after his appointment a crowd of peaceful demonstrators was fired upon by the police and many were killed. Romero protested to the leaders of the country.

Not long after, a Jesuit priest was murdered. He had been helping the very poorest in the country and was a friend of Romero. The archbishop protested again about the wickedness and cruelty of the regime.

His shyness and nervousness began to disappear as he bravely championed the cause of the poor and oppressed. He gave a weekly radio sermon that was eagerly listened to and he soon became a national figure.

But those in the extreme right- and left-wing parties could bear his stand for justice and truth no longer.

On 24 March 1980, Oscar

Archbishop Oscar Romero, a national figure in El Salvador, was shot in his own cathedral for speaking out against a cruel regime.

Romero was celebrating mass in the cathedral of San Salvador. He lifted the communion cup and spoke these words: 'May Christ's sacrifice give us the courage to offer our own bodies for justice and peace.'

At that moment a shot rang out through the quiet of the cathedral and Romero fell dead at the altar, the victim of an assassin's bullet.

TIME TO CHOOSE

After their last supper together, Jesus and his friends talked for a long time. Then they crossed the brook and went to the garden of Gethsemane, which lay on the other side of the valley. Silver-grey olive trees spread protective branches over their heads and the evening air was still.

But Jesus began to be dreadfully sad and distressed.

'Please stay with me,' he whispered to Peter and James and John. 'I must pray to my Father.'

Then Jesus went a little way from them and began to pray in great agony.

'Father,' they heard him say, 'if it is possible, rescue me from the bitter suffering that lies ahead. But only save me if that is part of your good plan. I want to please and obey you, not myself.'

Then the tired disciples fell asleep and heard no more.

Twice Jesus came back to them, needing their companionship and comfort, but both times they had nodded off to sleep.

The third time he returned, he said to them, 'Wake up now! My enemies are close.'

Every trace of drowsiness vanished when they heard the snap of twigs and the steady tread of approaching feet. Then they saw a bright line of torches bobbing through the darkness. Soon they made out the figures of soldiers and men armed with sticks. Judas walked at their head.

'Master!' he called out, and went up to Jesus, kissing him as if he were still his best friend.

At that signal the soldiers swarmed forward and held Jesus tight.

Peter brandished the sword he held and slashed at the High Priest's servant, slicing off his ear.

'Put your sword away, Peter,' Jesus said quietly. 'If I wished to be rescued I could call on vast armies of angels to defend me.'

Then Jesus gently healed the torn ear.

'Who are you looking for?' he asked the mob.

'Jesus of Nazareth,' they answered.

'I am he,' Jesus told them.

For a moment the soldiers fell back, cowed.

'I have told you that I am the person you want,' Jesus went on. 'Arrest me and let my friends go free.'

So the soldiers and Jewish police guards came forward again and seized him roughly. They tied him up and began to march him away to the High Priest's house.

JESUS' CHOICE

Eunice works as a Wycliffe Bible translator among the Mazatec Indians. One day she gave a piece of translation to José, a local helper, to check through. It was the story of Jesus' arrest.

When he got to the words, 'As soon as he said to them, "I am he," they went backward and fell to the ground,' Jose stopped reading and began to chuckle softly.

Eunice looked over his shoulder and re-read her translation. She thought that he must be amused by some mistake that she had made. But she could see nothing wrong. So she waited for him to explain.

'They could not have done a thing to Jesus without his permission,' Jose said happily. His chuckle had been one of joy because he realized that in spite of the armed soldiers, Jesus was never at the mercy of his enemies. He was in charge. He chose to die.

PETER'S CHOICE

When the soldiers seized Jesus and began to march him away, the terrified disciples took to their heels and ran. But Peter and John recovered their wits in time to see which way the little column was moving. They began to follow from a safe distance and saw the escort and their prisoner turn in at the entrance to the High Priest's house.

John had friends among the household, so he knocked boldly at the gate, then asked the servant girl if his friend could come in too. She nodded and beckoned for Peter to come inside the courtyard.

By this time, Jesus had been placed in front of a hastily assembled Council, whose members sat scrutinizing him in the hall that opened out of the central court. A rough and ready trial had already begun.

The girl at the gate looked hard at Peter. 'Aren't you a follower of the prisoner?' she asked, pointing at Jesus.

Peter's heart gave a violent lurch. 'Certainly not!' he blurted out quickly. He crossed to a glowing brazier that warmed the cool night air. A little group of men was clustered round it. They looked up as Peter came close.

'Here, you're a follower of that Jesus!' one of them exclaimed.

'No, I'm not!' Peter replied.

But one of the High Priest's servants peered into his face. 'I saw you with him in the garden,' he insisted.

In sudden panic Peter began to swear loudly, 'I don't even know the man!'

At that instant a cock crowed.

Peter remembered Jesus' words: 'Before you hear the cock crow, you will have said three times over that you don't know me.' A great wave of shame and self-disgust swept over him.

He looked across at the solitary figure who calmly faced his accusers.

Jesus turned and looked at Peter with love and understanding.

With a cry of despair, Peter rushed out of the courtyard, sobbing as if his heart would break.

Jesus in the Garden of Gethsemane: from the film Jesus of Nazareth.

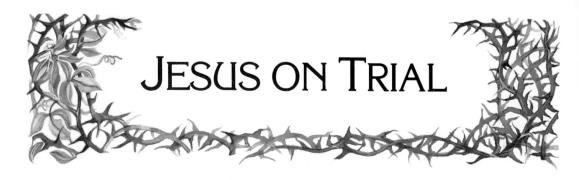

JESUS ON TRIAL

All night long, the High Priest, and the Council he presided over, tried in vain to bring a legal charge against Jesus. Under Jewish law, an accused person had to be found guilty of a crime by two separate witnesses before he could be convicted. Many different witnesses were produced to speak against Jesus, but none of them told the same tale. Jesus refused to defend himself against these trumped-up charges.

The High Priest grew desperate. How could he condemn Jesus legally? At last he put Jesus on oath and asked him:

'Are you the Messiah, the son of God?'

Jesus answered with complete certainty, 'Yes. The day will come when you will see me at God's right hand, coming with the clouds of heaven.'

The High Priest gave a gasp of horror. He and the whole Council recognized that Jesus was quoting words about the Messiah from the book of Daniel.

'There is no more to be said!' he exclaimed. 'This man has confessed to his own crime. He deserves to die for

claiming to be God's son.'

Jesus was handed over to the custody of rough and brutal soldiers.

TRIAL BY PILATE

Although the Jewish court had reached their verdict, they could not sentence Jesus to death. Only the Roman authorities had the power to order the death penalty. So the next task was to persuade Pilate, the Roman Governor, that Jesus was a threat to Roman rule and therefore deserved to die.

Pilate was staying in

Jesus stands trial before the High Priest: from the film Jesus of Nazareth.

Jerusalem during Passover week. The city was packed with excited pilgrims and tempers flared. The Governor must be at hand in case trouble broke out.

Early Friday morning, the Jewish Council sent representatives to Pilate, taking Jesus with them, in chains.

'This man says he is a king,' they reported. 'He tells people not to pay tax to Rome.'

Pilate looked at them shrewdly. He guessed that it was a trumped-up charge brought against Jesus out of jealousy. He began to question Jesus for himself.

'Are you really a king?' he asked curiously.

'My kingdom does not belong to this world,' Jesus answered. 'If it did, my subjects would be defending me. But my subjects do not go to war. My purpose in coming into the world is to speak the truth. Everyone who belongs to the truth listens to me.'

'What *is* truth?' Pilate asked.

He was certain now that Jesus was innocent and made up his mind to have the case dismissed. But the Jewish leaders had quickly rounded up a crowd of supporters and stationed them outside Pilate's residence.

As soon as Pilate came out and announced, 'The prisoner is innocent,' they began to chant, 'Crucify! Crucify!' over and over again.

Pilate tried once more. 'It's Passover, so I shall set a prisoner free to celebrate. Shall I release Jesus?'

'No!' they screamed back. 'We want Barabbas!' Barabbas had been thrown into prison for riot and murder.

Pilate's courage began to fail. If he insisted on releasing Jesus there would be trouble and violence in the streets of Jerusalem. He would have to answer for it to Rome. It would be far wiser to wash his hands of the whole affair. With a despairing shrug, he handed Jesus over to the Roman soldiers, first to be flogged and then to be crucified.

FALSE CHARGES

Rigged trials and unfair imprisonment are nothing new. All down the ages, to our own time, people of many nations and faiths have condemned innocent men and women unjustly.

In the USSR, both Jews and Christians are persecuted because of what they believe.

Valeri Barinov is a young musician.

'Jesus gave me a vision,' he wrote, 'to sound a trumpet call to Russia and to people all over the world.'

He has done so by writing a rock muscial, called *The Trumpet Call*, which he recorded in spite of tremendous difficulties, in both Russian and English. The record was smuggled to Britain and has since been recorded again by Dave Markee.

Barinov himself was tried and sentenced to serve in a labour camp. At his so-called trial, he said, 'My only crime is in being a Christian.'

MARK'S STORY

In 1984 when Mark, who is Polish, was ten years old, his father was put in prison for belonging to the free Trade Union movement Solidarity. Mark wrote this letter to his relatives:

'I did not know that they had taken my father away. I was asleep and I did not hear a thing. But my brother must have heard something because he was crying and Mummy was trying to pacify him. He is very small. He can barely talk. Next day our neighbour burst into tears when she saw me. She said that my dad was in prison for Solidarity. At first I was ashamed that my father was in prison and remembered that when the father of one of my classmates was put into prison for stealing, the other boys laughed at him and called him the "son of a thief".

'At school the teacher gave me some sausage and some money. She said that the money was for us and the sausage was for my father. I then told her that my father was not in prison but was travelling. And I started to cry. The teacher told me that I should not be ashamed, because it was not my father who was guilty, but the men who imprisoned him.'

THE DEATH OF ASLAN

In The Lion, the Witch and the Wardrobe, which is the first of the Narnia books, C. S. Lewis tells the story of Lucy and Susan and their brothers, Peter and Edmund. In the world which they discover beyond the wardrobe it is winter all the time, because the White Witch has usurped the power of the true ruler, Aslan the Lion. Edmund turns traitor and, to save him and all Narnia, Aslan gives his own life. Lucy and Susan follow Aslan as he makes his way to the Stone Table on the hill . . .

A great crowd of people were standing all round the Stone Table and though the moon was shining many of them carried torches which burned with evil-looking red flames and black smoke. But such people! Ogres with monstrous teeth, and wolves, and bull-headed men . . . Cruels and Hags and Incubuses, Wraiths, Horrors, Efreets, Sprites, Orknies, Wooses, and Ettins . . . And right in the middle, standing by the Table, was the Witch herself.

A howl and a gibber of dismay went up from the creatures when they first saw the great Lion pacing towards them, and for a moment even the Witch seemed to be struck with fear. Then she recovered herself and gave a wild fierce laugh.

'The fool!' she cried. 'The fool has come. Bind him fast.'

Lucy and Susan held their breaths waiting for Aslan's roar and his spring upon his enemies. But it never came. Four Hags, grinning and leering, yet also (at first) hanging back and half afraid of what they had to do, had approached him.

'Bind him, I say!' repeated the White Witch. The Hags made a dart at him and shrieked with triumph when they found that he made no resistance at all. Then others — evil dwarfs and apes — rushed in to help them, and between them they rolled the huge Lion over on his back and tied all his four paws together, shouting and cheering as if they had done something brave, though, had the Lion chosen, one of those paws could have been the death of them all. But he made no noise, even when the enemies, straining and tugging, pulled the cords so tight that they cut into his flesh. Then they began to drag him towards the Stone Table.

'Stop!' said the Witch. 'Let him first be shaved.'

Another roar of mean laughter went up from her followers as an ogre with a pair of shears came forward and squatted down by Aslan's head. Snip-snip-snip went the shears and masses of curling gold began to fall to the ground . . .

'Muzzle him!' said the Witch. And even now, as they worked about his face putting on the muzzle, one bite from his jaws would have cost two or three of them their hands. But he never moved. And this seemed to enrage all that rabble . . . For a few minutes the two girls could not even see him — so thickly was he surrounded by the whole crowd of creatures kicking him, hitting him, spitting on him, jeering at him.

At last the rabble had had enough of this. They began to drag the bound and muzzled Lion to the Stone Table, some pulling and some pushing. He was so huge that even when they got him there it took all their efforts to hoist him on to the surface of it. Then there was more tying and tightening of cords.

'The cowards! The cowards!' sobbed Susan. 'Are they *still* afraid of him, even now?'

When once Aslan had been tied (and tied so that he was really a mass of cords) on the flat stone, a hush fell on the crowd. Four Hags, holding four torches, stood at the corners of the Table. The Witch bared her arms . . . Then she began to whet her knife. It looked to the children, when the gleam of the torchlight fell on it, as if the knife were made of stone, not of steel, and it was of a strange and evil shape.

At last she drew near. She stood by Aslan's head. Her face was working and twitching with passion, but his looked up at the sky, still quiet, neither angry nor afraid, but a little sad. Then, just before she gave the blow, she stooped down and said in a quivering voice, 'And now, who has won?' . . .

The children did not see the actual moment of the killing. They couldn't bear to look and had covered their eyes.

If you turn to page 39 you can find out what happened next.

THE CRUCIFIXION

A purple robe, a crown of thorn,
A reed in his right hand;
Before the soldiers' spite and scorn
I see my Saviour stand.

He bears between the Roman guard
The weight of all our woe;
A stumbling figure bowed and scarred
I see my Saviour go.

Fast to the cross's spreading span,
High in the sunlit air,
All the unnumbered sins of man
I see my Saviour bear.

He hangs, by whom the world was made,
Beneath the darkened sky;
The everlasting ransom paid,
I see my Saviour die.

TIMOTHY DUDLEY-SMITH, 1968

The Roman soldiers led Jesus through the crowded streets of Jerusalem to the place of execution outside the city. The Romans crucified runaway slaves and the worst of criminals. It was a lingering and excruciatingly painful death.

Jesus was already weak from a night of interrogation and torture as well as from the Roman flogging, which was severe enough to cause death in itself. So the Roman officer in charge of the execution squad waylaid an African Jew, called Simon, and ordered him to carry the heavy wooden cross-beam for Jesus.

Some sympathetic women followed the little procession. They cried to see the kind, good Teacher going to his death.

Some of Jesus' close friends were there too. A few of the women, including Mary his mother, and John, one of the twelve disciples, stayed close to Jesus to the bitter end. Luke, the apostle Paul's doctor friend, describes Jesus' crucifixion in these words:

'Two other men, both of them criminals, were also led out to be put to death with Jesus. When they came to the place called "The Skull", they crucified Jesus there, and the two criminals, one on his right and the other on his left. Jesus said, "Forgive them, Father! They don't know what they are doing."

'They divided his clothes among themselves by throwing dice. The people stood there watching while the Jewish leaders jeered at him: "He saved others; let him save himself if he is the Messiah whom God has chosen!"

'The soldiers also mocked him: they came up to him and offered him cheap wine, and said, "Save yourself if you are the king of the Jews!"

'Above him were written these words: "This is the King of the Jews."

'One of the criminals hanging there hurled insults at him: "Aren't you the Messiah? Save yourself and us!"

'The other one, however, rebuked him, saying, "Don't you fear God? You received the same sentence he did. Ours, however, is only right, because we are getting what we deserve for what we did; but he has done no wrong." And he said to Jesus, "Remember me, Jesus, when you come as King!"

'Jesus said to him, "I promise you that today you will be in Paradise with me."

'It was about twelve o'clock when the sun stopped shining and darkness covered the whole country until three o'clock; and the curtain hanging in the Temple was torn in two. Jesus cried out in a loud voice, "Father! In your hands I place my spirit!" He said this and died.'
From LUKE'S GOSPEL, CHAPTER 23

'HE DIED TO SAVE US ALL'

Christians down the ages, who have realized Jesus' love in dying for them, have spent their lives telling others of his love.

GOD'S GADABOUT

Teresa was born in 1513, into an old Spanish family of Avila. When she was only thirteen, her mother died. Teresa grew up with her head stuffed with tales of chivalry and plans for marriage. But when her father sent her to a convent school to be educated, she began to hear God's call to the monastic life. Her father disapproved, so Teresa ran away from school to enter the Carmelite monastery at Avila.

At first she felt no nearer to God and had no peace of mind. Then, one day, when she was nearly forty years old, she saw a statue of Jesus, depicting him after he had been flogged by the Roman soldiers.

As she gazed at it she began to realize the full meaning of what he had suffered for her. She was deeply moved.

From that moment Teresa's life changed. She was able to say that although she often lost confidence in herself, she never lost confidence in God's great love and mercy to her.

Teresa made up her mind to reform the Carmelite order and to found new religious communities. She was always so busy visiting these convents that those who found her enthusiasm and efficiency inconvenient dubbed her a 'restless gadabout'.

But the books that she wrote on prayer, drawn from her own experience, show that her practical Christian living grew out of her personal meeting with Jesus and her response to his great love.

'A PLEASANT GARDEN OF THE LORD'

Count Nicholas Ludwig von Zinzendorf was born in Dresden in 1700. From childhood a deep love for Jesus filled his life. As a young aristocrat, he had to go to university and serve at court, but as soon as he could, he bought his grandmother's estate, so that he could make it 'a pleasant garden of the Lord', to give refuge to persecuted Christians of all denominations. The first arrivals were given a cow, to provide milk for their children, and timber to build a house.

From a growing community, missionaries went out to the whole world to tell the Good News of Jesus' love.

Zinzendorf wrote over 2,000 hymns, some still sung today. He was many years ahead of his time in seeking unity with all other Christians. He and his Moravian followers promised to 'love and own as brethren all children of God, let them belong to whatever denomination they may'.

Their watchword was 'the Lamb slain', the symbol of Jesus crucified for our sins. For when Zinzendorf was on the Grand Tour of Europe, at the age of nineteen, his attention was caught by a picture in the Dusseldorf Gallery by Domenico Feti, called 'Ecce Homo' (Behold the man).

It showed Jesus wearing the crown of thorns. Beneath it were the words, 'All this I did for thee; what doest thou for me?'

There and then Zinzendorf prayed to share Christ's suffering and to serve him faithfully.

Christian Finds Peace
by John Bunyan

Since the first Good Friday, when the criminal on the cross found forgiveness and peace through faith in Jesus, millions have found freedom from guilt through Jesus' death. John Bunyan describes the experience in his famous allegory about the Christian life, called The Pilgrim's Progress.

Now I saw in my dream, that the highway up which Christian was to go, was fenced on either side with a Wall, and that Wall is called Salvation. Up this way therefore did burdened Christian run, but not without great difficulty, because of the load on his back.

He ran thus till he came at a place somewhat ascending; and upon that place stood a Cross, and a little below in the bottom, a sepulchre. So I saw in my dream, that just as Christian came up with the Cross, his burden loosed from off his shoulders, and fell from off his back; and began to tumble, and so continued to do till it came to the mouth of the sepulchre, where it fell in, and I saw it no more.

Then was Christian glad and lightsome, and said with a merry heart, 'He hath given me rest, by his sorrow, and life, by his death.' Then he stood still a while, to look and wonder; for it was very surprising to him that the sight of the Cross should thus ease him of his burden. He looked therefore, and looked again, even till the springs that were in his head sent the waters down his cheeks. Now as he stood looking and weeping, behold three Shining Ones came to him, and saluted him, with 'Peace be to thee.' So the first said to him, 'Thy sins be forgiven.' The second stripped him of his rags, and clothed him with a change of raiment. The third also set a mark on his forehead, and gave him a roll with a seal upon it, which he bid him look on as he ran, and that he should give it in at the celestial Gate: so they went their way. Then Christian gave three leaps for joy, and went on singing,

> 'Thus far did I come loaden with my sin,
> Nor could aught ease the grief that I was in,
> Till I came hither. What a place is this!
> Must here be the beginning of my bliss?
> Must here the burden fall from off my back?
> Must here the strings that bound it to me,
>   crack?
> Blessed Cross! Blessed Sepulchre!
>   Blessed rather be
> The man that there was put to shame for me.'

At the beginning of The Pilgrim's Progress *Christian sets out on his journey, weighed down by the burden of his sins.*

DARK WAITING TIME

Jesus taught his disciples, ' "The Son of Man will be handed over to men who will kill him. Three days later, however, he will rise to life." But they did not understand what this teaching meant, and they were afraid to ask him.'
From MARK'S GOSPEL, CHAPTER 9

It was nine o'clock in the morning when Jesus was put on the cross. At noon, a strange darkness blotted out the fierce brightness of the sun. Then, at three o'clock, Jesus called out in a loud voice, 'It is finished!' and gave up his life.

The Roman execution squad was used to waiting many weary hours and even days for their victims to die. The officer in charge was amazed at what he had seen and heard.

'This man really was the Son of God!' he exclaimed.

The dead bodies of criminals were usually piled into a mass grave. But there were two men determined that Jesus' body should not be treated like that. They were both wealthy and influential leaders.

One, called Joseph, was a member of the Council. He had kept his loyalty to Jesus a secret, but he had refused to vote him 'guilty' at the trial. Now he bravely asked Pilate's permission to have Jesus' body.

Nicodemus, another secret follower of Jesus, who had once talked the night away with him, helped Joseph with the task.

They gently bathed the body and, before wrapping it in a linen shroud, they embalmed it with quantities of perfumes and spices. Then they carried it to a nearby garden, where Joseph owned a tomb.

They put the body on the rock shelf, inside the grave chamber cut out of solid rock. Then they rolled a huge stone in front of the tomb's mouth, to seal up the entrance.

Some of the women who had followed Jesus to the cross, watched silently. Then, full of sadness, their tears falling, they left the garden. There was nothing more that they could do.

SABBATH REST

The Jewish Sabbath begins at sunset on Friday. In obedience to God's commandment through Moses, no work was done and no shops were open on that day. The women longed to buy their own offering of spices and perfumes for Jesus' body, but they knew that they must wait until the Sabbath ended. They could only sit still until the longest day that they had ever known should draw to its close.

SUSAN AND LUCY WAIT TOO

Once the wicked White Witch, in the book
The Lion, the Witch and the Wardrobe by
C. S. Lewis, had killed Aslan, she mustered all
her forces to march against the human
children and all good creatures of Narnia. She
thought that she had won the battle. Susan
and Lucy thought so too, as they waited
through the long, dark night. But the promise
of morning and new life was at hand . . .

As soon as the wood was silent again Susan
and Lucy crept out into the open hill-top. The
moon was getting low and thin clouds were
passing across her, but still they could see the
shape of the Lion lying dead in his bonds. And
down they both knelt in the wet grass and
kissed his cold face and stroked his beautiful
fur — what was left of it — and cried till they
could cry no more. And then they looked at
each other and held each other's hands for
mere loneliness and cried again; and then
again were silent. At last Lucy said, 'I can't
bear to look at that horrible muzzle. I wonder
could we take it off?'

So they tried. And after a lot of working at
it (for their fingers were cold and it was now
the darkest part of the night) they succeeded.
And when they saw his face without it they
burst out crying again and kissed it and
fondled it and wiped away the blood and the
foam as well as they could. And it was all more
lonely and hopeless and horrid than I know
how to describe.

'I wonder could we untie him as well?' said
Susan presently. But the enemies, out of pure
spitefulness, had drawn the cords so tight that
the girls could make nothing of the knots.

I hope no one who reads this book has
been quite as miserable as Susan and Lucy
were that night; but if you have been — if
you've been up all night and cried till you have
no more tears left in you — you will know that
there comes in the end a sort of quietness. You
feel as if nothing was ever going to happen
again. At any rate that was how it felt to these
two. Hours and hours seemed to go by in this
dead calm, and they hardly noticed that they
were getting colder and colder. But at last Lucy
noticed two things. One was that the sky on
the east side of the hill was a little less dark
than it had been an hour ago. The other was
some tiny movement going on in the grass at
her feet. At first she took no interest in this.
What did it matter? Nothing mattered now! But
at last she saw that whatever-it-was had begun
to move up the upright stones of the Stone
Table. And now whatever-they-were were
moving about on Aslan's body. She peered
closer. They were little grey things.

'Ugh!' said Susan from the other side of
the Table. 'How beastly! There are horrid little
mice crawling over him. Go away, you little
beasts.' And she raised her hand to frighten
them away.

'Wait!' said Lucy, who had been looking at
them more closely still. 'Can you see what
they're doing?'

Both girls bent down and stared.

'I do believe —' said Susan. 'But how
queer! They're nibbling away at the cords!'

'That's what I thought,' said Lucy. 'I think
they're friendly mice. Poor little things — they
don't realize he's dead. They think it'll do
some good untying him.'

It was quite definitely brighter by now.
Each of the girls noticed for the first time the
white face of the other. They could see the
mice nibbling away; dozens and dozens, even
hundreds, of little field mice. And at last, one
by one, the ropes were all gnawed through . . .

The girls cleared away the remains of the
gnawed ropes. Aslan looked more like himself
without them. Every moment his dead face
looked nobler, as the light grew and they could
see it better.

In the wood behind them a bird gave a
chuckling sound. It had been so still for hours
and hours that it startled them. Then another
bird answered it. Soon there were birds singing
all over the place.

JESUS IS ALIVE!

The strife is o'er, the battle done,
The victory of life is won,
The song of triumph has begun: Hallelujah!

The powers of death have done their worst,
But Christ their legions hath dispersed;
Let shouts of holy joy outburst; Hallelujah!

The three sad days have quickly sped:
He rises glorious from the dead;
All glory to our risen Head: Hallelujah!

TWELFTH-CENTURY(?) LATIN HYMN
'Hallelujah' is Hebrew for 'Praise God!'

In spite of all that Jesus had told them beforehand, none of the disciples expected to see Jesus alive. It was only when they saw him with their own eyes that they believed the good news. The four Gospels describe their experiences. You can find the stories for yourself in Matthew's Gospel, chapter 28, verses 1-9; Mark 16:1-8; Luke 24:1-49; John 20:21.

SALOME'S STORY

'It was still dark when we set off to go to the tomb that Sunday morning. There was me and Joanna and the two Marys. We were taking spices to put on Jesus' body. How we thought we'd manage to get that huge stone rolled away from the cave entrance, I'm sure I don't know, but when we arrived in the garden we saw at once that someone else had moved it already. And that wasn't the biggest surprise we got. There, sitting on the stone was a bright, shining creature, so dazzling it hurt your eyes to look at him.

'Mary reckons there were two of them standing there and she may be right. We all agreed on one thing. Only an angel could look that bright and splendid.

'He spoke to us. "Don't be scared," he said. "I know you're looking for Jesus. But you're looking in the wrong place. He's not in the tomb. He's alive. Just you go and tell that to Peter and the others."

'We didn't wait to hear any more. We were scared out of our wits. Joanna and me and the other Mary just took to our heels and ran, and didn't stop running till we were out of the garden.

'But it was a different matter that evening. We saw him for ourselves then and I knew for certain. Jesus, our Master, is alive!'

MARY MAGDALENE'S STORY

'I didn't run away with the other women. I was so miserable to think that someone had taken away our Master's body, that I went on standing there, crying. I didn't even turn round when I heard someone ask me what the matter was.

'Then I thought perhaps he was the gardener and he

might be the one who had taken the body away. So I asked him to tell me where he'd put it. His answer was a single word — "Mary!"

'I knew that voice! I spun round and saw him. It was Jesus, my Master, alive from death.'

JOHN'S STORY

'When the women visited the tomb and found the stone rolled away, they came running to find Peter and me. We ran to the garden as fast as we could and, being younger and lighter on my feet, I got there first.

'But it was Peter who came panting up and went right inside the tomb. So I followed.

'The rock shelf on which Jesus' body had been placed was bare, except for the linen that had been wrapped round the corpse. I noticed that the head band lay by itself, just where the head had been. In a flash it dawned on me what had happened. The tomb was empty because Jesus was alive.'

Doubt padlocked one door and Memory put her back to the other. Still the damp draught seeped in though Fear chinked all the cracks and Blindness boarded up the window. In the darkness that was left Defeat crouched in his cold corner. Then Jesus came (all the doors being shut) and stood among them.
LUCI SHAW, 'A Widening Light'

THOMAS' STORY

'There was great excitement that first Sunday evening — or so they told me. I wasn't there, and missed it all. They had been huddling together behind locked doors — in case the authorities got hold of *them*. Suddenly, so they said, Jesus appeared, without anyone even opening the door. He said, "Peace to you."

'I told them they'd seen a ghost. "We thought so too at first," they agreed, "but the Master shared our supper. He was real, all right."

'I still wasn't convinced, not after the terrible way we'd seen him die. "I'd have to touch the very places where those nails went if I was to believe," I told them.

'It was one week later — same day, same place — but I was with them that time. Suddenly, without warning, just like they'd said, Jesus was with us. He looked straight at me and said, "Reach out and touch my hands and side, Thomas, as you said you must, if you were to believe. Don't go on doubting."

'I didn't need those proofs. I felt bitterly ashamed of my doubts, but gloriously happy that Jesus was alive. All I could do was to blurt out, "My Lord and my God!"

' "You believe because you've seen me with your eyes," the Master said. "Happy are the people who will believe in me without ever having seen me." '

At dawn on Easter Day the stone which sealed the tomb of Jesus was rolled away. Jesus had passed from death to life.

'He made them touch him and handle him to prove that he was really there; and then, when they seemed a little slow in the uptake, he ate some food, for who ever heard of a ghost making a hearty meal? He had said he would conquer death, and here he was alive and well to prove it.'
J. B. PHILLIPS

FLOWERS AND GARDENS

Cheer up, friends and neighbours,
Now it's Eastertide;
Stop from endless labours,
Worries put aside:
Men should rise from sadness,
Evil, folly, strife,
When God's mighty gladness
Brings the earth to life.

On Good Friday the church is bare but on Saturday many hands are busy preparing flowers for Easter Day. The flowers used will vary from one country to another, but yellow and white and green are favourite colours for the main display.

The arum lily is a traditional Easter flower but in the USA another type of lily was transplanted from Bermuda because it flowers at the right time.

In Sweden it is also the custom to bring tight-budded branches of flowering trees into the house some weeks beforehand, so that they will bloom indoors for Easter. Sometimes they are made into little Easter trees and the branches hung with coloured eggs, real or ornamental. In Norway they pick birch or willow and sometimes decorate the branches with coloured feathers.

THE GARDEN TOMB

Donald Bridge was Chaplain of the Garden Tomb in Jerusalem. No one knows the actual site of Jesus' crucifixion and burial but, over a hundred years ago, the British soldier General Gordon was convinced that he had found the place. The ground around the ancient tomb was bought and the sepulchre excavated.

The garden today includes an open-air amphitheatre where services can be held. About a thousand people visit the tomb every day. Children on a school cruise rub shoulders with UN soldiers, and Africans and Japanese mingle with Americans and Europeans. Every Sunday a service is held in the garden and on Easter Day thousands join in the sunrise service to celebrate Jesus' resurrection.

But this pilgrimage to a tomb is different from any other. Every Sunday the tomb is closed and a little door fastened to the entrance, on which are the angel's words: 'He is not here, he is risen!'

When Don took pilgrims to see the tomb, he used to say, 'In the long run, it doesn't really matter whether this is the authentic tomb or not, because of three simple words that sum it up: "It is empty!" '

FLOWERS IN THE CHURCHYARD
by Francis Kilvert

On Easter Eve, country folk in Wales used to decorate their family graves. Francis Kilvert, who was curate in Clyro, described in his diary for Easter Saturday 1870 the scene in his churchyard:

People kept arriving from all parts with flowers to dress the graves. Children were coming from the town and from neighbouring villages with baskets of flowers and knives to cut holes in the turf. The roads were lively with people coming and going and the churchyard a busy scene with women and children and a few men moving about among the tombstones and kneeling down beside the green mounds flowering the graves . . .

More and more people kept coming into the churchyard as they finished their day's work. The sun went down in glory behind the dingle, but still the work of love went on through the twilight and into the dusk until the moon rose full and splendid. The figures continued to move about among the graves and to bend over the green mounds in the calm clear moonlight and warm air of the balmy evening.

At eight o'clock there was a gathering of the choir in the church to practise the two anthems for tomorrow. The moonlight came streaming in broadly through the chancel windows. When the choir had gone and the lights were out and the church quiet again, as I walked down the churchyard alone the decked graves had a strange effect in the moonlight and looked as if the people had laid down to sleep for the night out of doors, ready dressed to rise early on Easter morning . . . The air was as soft and warm as a summer night, and the broad moonlight made the quiet village almost as light as day. Everyone seemed to have gone to rest and there was not a sound except the clink and trickle of the brook.

MAKING AN EASTER GARDEN

Line a shallow dish with garden soil or potting compost and cover the soil with moss. Scrape a space in the centre of the dish large enough for a small container such as an egg cup. Fill it with water and an arrangement of small flowers and leaves. Choose flowers that are in season in your country, whether spring or autumn ones. Decorate the garden in any other way you like. Spray the moss with water to keep it fresh

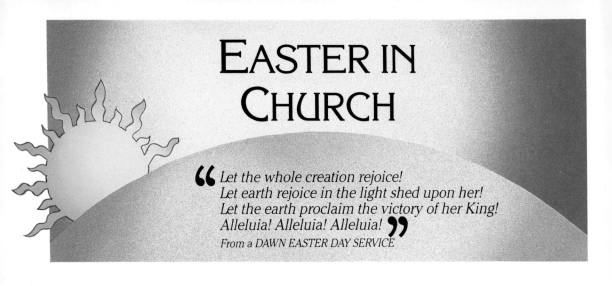

EASTER IN CHURCH

“ Let the whole creation rejoice!
Let earth rejoice in the light shed upon her!
Let the earth proclaim the victory of her King!
Alleluia! Alleluia! Alleluia! ”
From a DAWN EASTER DAY SERVICE

Perhaps more people go to church on Easter Day than on any other Sunday in the year. Easter was the earliest Christian festival to be celebrated and in the Eastern church it is still the most important.

In earlier centuries, new converts were baptized on Easter Eve and a midnight vigil of dedication followed. Some services still begin at midnight, others at dawn. In many churches services are at the normal Sunday time, but are transformed by the joyful singing of all the best loved Easter hymns.

During Passion week — the week in which Good Friday comes — the candles in many churches are gradually extinguished. The last, central candle is finally put out and placed behind the altar. The betrayal and death of Jesus is at hand and the church is left in darkness.

On Easter Eve new fire is struck from flint and steel and used to light three candles. From these the Paschal candle is lighted, symbol of the risen Lord. In past centuries Paschal candles in cathedrals were immense. There are records of the huge quantities of wax required to make them. People came from far and near to see the huge candle at Durham Cathedral in England. It rose twelve times the height of a man, reaching almost to the roof, from where it had to be lit.

ST PATRICK'S NEW FIRE

At the time of the great Celtic festival of fire, to celebrate the rebirth of life at springtime, the fire on every hearth had to be extinguished. Then all were relit from the sacred flame of new fire kindled at Tara in Ireland, where the High King held court.

Once, according to legend, St Patrick resolved to keep Easter at Tara. Before the light from the High King's fire leapt across the plain, the Paschal fire lighted by Patrick glowed from the hill-top of Slane. Not all the raging of the High King and his druids could quench it. The light of Christ had conquered the darkness of pagan superstition and magic.

Christians in Korea meet for a dawn service on Easter Day.

MIDNIGHT IN MOSCOW
by Michael Bourdeaux

Michael Bourdeaux is Director of Keston College in England, a centre which monitors religious belief in Eastern Europe and the USSR. Nearly thirty years ago, as a student in Moscow, he celebrated Easter at a midnight service in the city . . .

I was standing in the church in total darkness. Although I was protected in a little enclosure at the front I knew the church must be full, not only because we had had to shoulder through twelve thousand people shut outside by calling out *inostrantsy* (foreigners), not because any murmur of a multitude broke the silence, but because I could feel the tension, the spiritual expectancy, if you like, which the faithful generated.

Sometimes at Orthodox Easter there was trouble. This often affected first the procession going around the outside of the church at the very beginning of the service, symbolically looking for the body of Christ . . . This year there was calm. The sound of a distant, mournful chant. It grew louder as the deacons and priests approached the main door: 'They have taken away my Lord and I know not where they have laid him.'

A hammering and creaking from the back indicated a great door opening. 'Whom seek ye?' 'The body of Jesus.' 'Why seek ye the living among the dead? He is not here. He is risen — *Khristos voskrese!*' For the first time the great crowd broke its silence. A murmur, as though they could not believe the truth they were affirming: *Voistinu voskrese* ('Is risen indeed') was their antiphon. But now too there was light. Someone at the back had lit the first paschal candle, a single point of light not able to penetrate the darkness. But then there was another, and another. Swiftly the flame passed from hand to hand. I began to see what I had not known. Every one of the worshippers held a candle. In less than a minute the church was a blaze of light — no, not the impersonal glare of electricity — it was five thousand individual flames united in one faith. Each candle lit up a face behind it. That face bore the deep lines of sorrow, of personal tragedy. Yet, as it was illuminated, the suffering turned to joy, to the certain knowledge of the reality of the risen Lord. Seeing my empty hands, an old lady reached out to me across the low rail. I could hardly hear her say, *Khristos voskrese* above the exultant shouts that now came from the worshippers, but as I replied I felt the barriers of nationality and culture fall away. I was one of them.

In Eastern Europe Christians carrying torches celebrate the resurrection of Jesus on Easter Day.

LOOKING AT THE EVIDENCE

66 Many lawyers have considered the evidence for believing that Jesus rose again, and have concluded that this evidence is stronger than most that is used in courts of law. The nature of the eye-witness reports, including their slight contradiction on points of detail, is exactly as an experienced lawyer would expect to find it. 99

From JESUS THEN AND NOW,
by David Watson and Simon Jenkins

There is plenty of good evidence for believing that Jesus rose from death. If he did not, what became of his body? His enemies would certainly have found it and displayed it as proof that the disciples were mistaken. But another strong piece of evidence is the number of people who saw Jesus alive. St Paul, writing only about twenty years after the event, mentions some of these witnesses by name and states that on one occasion more than 500 saw Jesus. Most of them, he said, were still alive when he wrote and could have been cross-questioned.

DOES IT MATTER?

St Paul makes it clear that it is very important indeed to believe that Jesus rose from death. Without a Saviour and Leader who has defeated death and evil and is alive today, there is no Christian good news to tell.

'If Christ has not been raised from death, then we have nothing to preach and you have nothing to believe . . . If Christ has not been raised, then your faith is a delusion and you are still lost in your sins. It would also mean that the believers in Christ who have died are lost. If our hope in Christ is good for this life only and no more, then we deserve more pity than anyone else in all the world.

'But the truth is that Christ has been raised from death, as the guarantee that those who sleep in death will also be raised. For just as death came by means of a man, in the same way the rising from death comes by means of a man. For just as all people die because of their union with Adam, in the same way all will be raised to life because of their union with Christ.'
From 1 CORINTHIANS 15

WHO MOVED THE STONE?

Over fifty years ago, a journalist, Frank Morison, wrote a book called *Who Moved the Stone?* In his first chapter, entitled 'The Book that Refused to be Written', he describes how he set out to write about the last days in Jesus' life, convinced that the Gospel records were unreliable and that the resurrection never took place.

Although he admired Jesus, he drew the line at miracles. But, as he began to look closely at the evidence, he found it too convincing to dismiss. The book that had been planned to contradict Christian belief in the resurrection, became a powerfully reasoned document in its defence.

MAN ALIVE

Michael Green, in a book called *Man Alive*, imagines a conversation with the 500 disciples who saw Jesus alive.

' "Are you concerned to say that on a certain day you saw Jesus alive after his death? Is *that* it?" we might ask. "No," they would reply, "that is not the main point. On such and such a day we did indeed meet Jesus, alive again from the tomb. But to us the greatest thing is that he is with us still, though we cannot see him. He shares our very lives. He talks with us and we with him every day. He has come by his Holy Spirit to take up residence in our personalities. He is no past hero to us. He is our living contemporary and companion. Our great aim is to allow him to control and transform our characters, and to use us in introducing others to God." '

Michael Green goes on to describe his own meeting with Jesus:

'I had believed in the fact of the resurrection, in a second-hand way, all my life; but it meant nothing to me in practice. . . A friend showed me that if Jesus rose, then it followed that he was alive. So I could meet him, and come to know him. Hesitantly, then, I put my life in his hands, as best I knew how. And I have proved the reality of his presence ever since. It has gradually become the greatest certainty of my life.'

'There is a great gulf between the demoralised disciples after the crucifixion, huddled behind locked doors, fearful and bewildered, and the world transformers that Peter and the rest became, willing to die for the truth of what they had seen — Jesus Christ raised to life. It was Jesus who led the disciples out of shock into faith.'

DR RUNCIE,
ARCHBISHOP OF CANTERBURY,
Easter Day, 1985

The earliest surviving New Testament document is a fragment of John's Gospel written less than a century after Jesus' death.

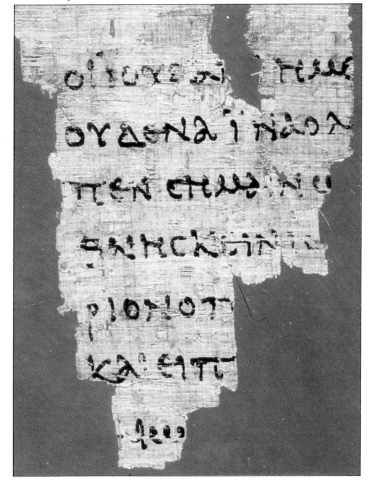

EASTER EGGS

Easter eggs! Easter eggs!
Give to him that begs!
For Christ the Lord is arisen.

To the poor, open door,
something give from your store!
For Christ the Lord is arisen.

Those who hoard, can't afford —
moth and rust their reward!
For Christ the Lord is arisen.

Those who love freely give —
long and well may they live!
For Christ the Lord is arisen.

Eastertide, like a bride,
comes, and won't be denied.
For Christ the Lord is arisen.

RUSSIAN EASTER CAROL

As that old carol suggests, at one time boys and girls did not wait to be given eggs for Easter. They went around asking for them. Country people were usually only too glad to give them some. For the long weeks of Lent, the church had forbidden them to eat eggs — but the hens went on laying! So there were plenty of eggs to be used up once Easter arrived.

Even before Christian times, gifts of eggs were exchanged at spring time.

Greeks, Chinese and Persians all gave one another eggs to celebrate new life in nature. For Christians the egg became a picture of Jesus rising to new life from his dark tomb.

In the Middle Ages kings would give presents of eggs at Easter. There is an entry for eighteen pence, in the royal accounts of 1290, when the English King Edward bought 450 eggs to give to members of his household. But first the eggs were to be covered with gold leaf!

In many countries eggs were painted red — in memory of Christ's blood, some say.

PRECIOUS EGGS

Louis XIV, the splendid 'Sun King' of France, ordered artists to paint beautiful scenes on the eggs that he gave to his friends. After his time, ostrich eggs, from the zoo at Versailles, were painted as gifts for the king himself. Then French craftsmen began to make eggs from all kinds of precious materials — gold, ivory and fine porcelain. Some of these eggs were surprise ones — they could be opened to reveal a jewelled present inside.

The most famous precious eggs were made by the Russian goldsmith, Fabergé, for his royal clients. Tsar Alexander III ordered the first one for the Tsarina. Fabergé made it of white enamel. It opened, and inside was a gold 'yolk'. The yolk contained a tiny gold hen

In many countries eggs are painted or dyed as Easter gifts.

with ruby eyes. Inside the hen was a miniature imperial crown, made of diamonds.

For many years Fabergé made at least one egg every Easter for the ruling Tsar and every year it was different. Altogether he created fifty-seven eggs, treasured now in palaces and museums throughout the world.

Among less wealthy people in Russia, painted wooden eggs became popular. In other regions, brilliantly decorated and lacquered eggs of papier maché were made.

EGGS PAINTED AND DYED

Since the Middle Ages people have been decorating eggs for Easter gifts. The eggs had first to be hard boiled or the raw white and yolk removed by 'blowing' them through a tiny hole.

Vegetable dyes were used and, by first tracing patterns with melted wax, it was possible to block the effect of the dye, leaving a design once the wax was removed.

Patterns could be painted on the eggs too. In every Polish village there were women who specialized in decorating eggs and had their own geometric designs. Some painted on the Christian symbols of the fish or the cross.

In Hungary eggs were often decorated with red flowers on a white ground. In Yugoslavia they were marked with the letters XV, which stood for 'Christos vakrese' or 'Christ is risen'.

EGGS TO MAKE

Chocolate eggs were not made until the very end of the nineteenth century. Instead of buying them for presents this year, why not paint or dye some hens' eggs yourself? There are many different ways of doing so. Acrylic paint takes well on hardboiled eggs. Here is one simple and successful method of dyeing eggs.

You will need
Eggs — at room temperature
some outside onion skins
(red onion skins as well as brown ones if available)
old nylon tights to cut up.

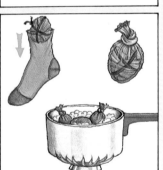

1
Wrap the onion skins around the eggs — it doesn't matter about doing this too evenly — there can be gaps.

2
Tie the skins in place with some strips from the tights.

3
For extra safety, put each egg into the cut-off foot of a tight, knotting the material above, to keep it in place.

4
Boil the eggs. Use warm water, bring slowly to boil then boil gently for forty minutes at least.

5
Remove the eggs and leave to cool.

6
Unwrap them — the exciting bit!

7
Using a soft cloth, rub a little oil into the still-warm eggs to make them shiny and bright.

THE UNEXPECTED TRAVELLER

Two of Jesus' followers knew nothing about the glad event of Easter Day, when they left Jerusalem that Sunday evening, as Luke's Gospel records. They were going to Emmaus, a village two hours' walk from the city. As they went, they talked over the terrible happenings of the past week.

'I had such high hopes,' Cleopas said for the hundredth time. 'I was sure that Jesus was God's Messiah, come to save and rescue us.'

'Yes,' his companion agreed, 'but we were wrong. He's been dead three days now, so there's an end to our dreams.'

They were so wrapped up in their misery that they scarcely noticed the approaching steps of another traveller. But when he came close, he slowed down to walk beside them.

'You're looking very miserable,' he began, in a friendly voice, 'what's the matter?'

'Do you mean that you haven't heard what's been going on in Jerusalem?' they asked him. Then they poured out their story.

To their surprise, he did not share their disappointment.

'How foolish you are!' he said. 'Don't you see that there has been no mistake?' Then the stranger reminded them of one Old Testament passage after another that told of God's age-old plan for his Messiah to suffer and die and rise to life again. That is how he would save his own Jewish people and all mankind.

The time flew by as the stranger talked and, as darkness fell, they arrived at their own doorstep.

'Come in!' they begged, and the stranger joined them for their simple supper.

As he took the bread, thanked God for it, and shared it out between them, they recognized him. Their unknown companion was Jesus himself, alive from death! They looked at each other in wonder and joy, but when they turned to speak to Jesus, he had gone.

All tiredness vanished, they raced back to Jerusalem, to share the good news with Jesus' other friends.

God's Suffering Servant

We have a good idea which passages from the Old Testament were included in Jesus' explanations to the disciples. In the Gospels and the book of Acts, Jesus and the apostles refer to particular writings which describe Jesus' coming and his kind of kingship. Here is one of them:

Who would have believed what we have heard?
Where has God's power ever been seen —
    but here?
He grew up among us, like a sapling —
    like a plant rooted in dry ground.
So he had no beauty
    no splendour to attract us,
    no grace to charm us.
Spurned and withdrawing from human society,
    he was a man who suffered;
    pain was his close acquaintance.
Like one who must hide his face from us
    he was despised;
    we held him of no account.
And yet —
they were our sufferings that weighed on him;
    our pains were the burden he bore.
While we —
We counted him smitten by God,
    struck down by God,
    humiliated by God!
But he —
he was pierced by our rebellions,
    crushed by our misdeeds;
his burden was the suffering that made us
    whole,
    he endured pain that brought healing
      to us.
While we —
we were the guilty;
    we had strayed like sheep,
    each going his own way.
But God!
God burdened him
    with the punishment for the guilt of us all.
He was oppressed;
    he was struck down.

He said nothing.
He was taken away —
    like a sheep to slaughter
    like a ewe to the shearers.
He said nothing.
He was silent.
He was arrested;
    he was sentenced.
He was taken away;
    no one raised a protest at his fate.
He was cut off from the land of life,
    struck down because of the guilt of his
      people.
He was assigned a grave with the wicked,
    a burial place with criminals —
for he had practised non-violence,
    and had never spoken dishonestly!
It is God who purposes the suffering;
    God puts him to grief.
When his life is offered for the guilt of others,
    he sees his offspring,
    he gains vitality,
    by him the Lord's plans prosper.
After he has drunk deep of affliction,
    is satiated with suffering,
he is proved innocent before the multitudes,
    it is their guilt he bears.
So I rank him among the great,
    and he may take a hero's portion,
because he exposed himself to death,
    letting himself be taken as a sinner;
and all the while he was suffering the guilt of
      many,
    and intervening for wrongdoers.

ISAIAH 53, translated from the Hebrew by Professor D. J. A. Clines

EASTER CELEBRATIONS

Long before Jesus died and rose again at Easter, people used to celebrate the return of new life at springtime. Many special Christian customs have been added to the ones that were already firm favourites, but more often the pagan customs have been given a Christian meaning.

FOOD

After the lean months of winter and fast weeks of Lent, food at Easter was always a special treat. Roast lamb with mint sauce was the traditional main course, followed by custard tarts sprinkled with currants and flat Easter biscuits.

CLOTHES

In a number of countries it is still the custom to wear at least one new thing to celebrate Easter. It used to be thought very unlucky not to wear new clothes at Easter. Some say the custom began when those baptized at Easter put on new white clothes to represent the new life they had begun. Everyone else joined in and wore new clothes too, to remind them of their own baptism vows. But the custom may go back to pagan times.

GAMES

For many centuries boys and girls in many lands have played special games with hard-boiled eggs. Sometimes a crowd will gather at the top of a hill to roll the eggs down — and see which one is last to crack. Some say it is in memory of the stone rolled away from Jesus' tomb.

In the USA, as many as 10,000 people arrive at the White House, where they are allowed to roll their eggs across the President's own lawns, in a competition to see whose egg goes furthest. Adults are allowed in only if they are accompanied by a child!

In other places, boys play a game like 'conkers'. The aim is to crack your opponent's egg by knocking it with your own. In France, the eggs were thrown up in the air and caught. The boy who dropped his egg had to pay a forfeit.

Real or sugar eggs are sometimes hidden for children to find. They say that the Easter hare has hidden them. The hare was connected with the worship of the Anglo-Saxon goddess Eostre, whose festival was in spring. In some countries the children prepare little nests in the garden, ready for the Easter hare to put their eggs.

Because hares and rabbits are a bit alike the Easter rabbit has also come onto the scene, by mistake!

But in France the children are told that it is the church bells — silent from Maundy Thursday to Easter morning — that have been to Rome to fetch them their eggs.

FAIRS AND PARADES

There are processions through the streets of many Spanish cities from Palm Sunday onwards. Floats with scenes depicting the Bible stories are carried through the streets, while bare-footed penitents walk alongside. But when Easter comes the mood changes. Everyone puts on best clothes and prepares to enjoy the spring fair or *feria*. The *feria* in Seville is one of the largest in the world. The singing and dancing go on for days.

Ladies used to stroll up

and down in Battersea Park, in London, to show off their new Easter hats. Now the Easter Bonnet parade has become a large procession with floats and brass bands. There is a parade of people wearing new clothes along New York's Fifth Avenue too.

BEFORE AND AFTER

In Sweden the children go round in disguise on Easter Eve, delivering special Easter greeting letters and letting off fireworks and crackers in the streets. In many countries bonfires are lighted that evening.

In Sicily the celebration begins on Easter Eve too. They say that it is because they are nearer the Holy Land and heard the news first. But the Italians say it is because Sicilians just can't wait!

Easter Monday is a holiday too. Before the days of annual holidays of several weeks, a day off was a great occasion. All kinds of races and sports meetings were arranged for that day. Some very strange local games are played too, most going back to pre-Christian times.

THE JUBILANT SUN

Even the sun rejoices on Easter Day, they say. According to Celtic legend it dances for joy. One old Highland woman claimed to have seen it — just once in her life. She said: 'The glorious gold-bright sun was after rising on the crest of the great hill and it was changing colour — green, purple, red, blood-red, white, intense white and gold-white, like the glory of the God of the

elements to the children of men. It was dancing up and down in exultation at the joyous resurrection of the beloved Saviour of victory.'

Swedish children dress in disguise to deliver Easter greetings.

CHICKEN BUNS FOR EASTER

In Norway they make chicken buns for Easter. Recipes using yeast are sometimes difficult, but ready-prepared sachets of yeast-mix make it simple.

To make about 12 chicks you will need:
1jb/450g strong bread flour
1 teaspoon of salt
about ½ pint/300ml of lukewarm milk (comfortable to the finger!) small knob of butter, melted easy-bake yeast: quantity as instructed on the sachet

1
Work it all together into a dough and knead vigorously for about 10 minutes.

2
Divide into 12 equal pieces. Roll each piece into a nice fat 'snake' about 4 inches/10cm long.

3
Make a knot of each 'snake' as shown in the pictures.

4
Push in two currants for eyes and a piece of red glacé cherry for a beak.

5
Place on a greased baking sheet and cover with a piece of greased polythene. Leave in a warm place until they double in size. This may take an hour.

6
Brush gently with beaten egg and bake in a very hot oven for 5-10 minutes.

Here are your chickens. You'll love them!

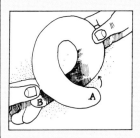
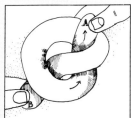

LOVE IS COME AGAIN

Peter was desperately unhappy. He had left Jesus in the lurch when he was taken prisoner in the garden, then protested three times over that he did not know him. It seemed as if nothing would wash away the stain of that dreadful night. But now he had seen Jesus alive again, and hope began to grow.

One night Peter and his companions went fishing and when they returned in the early light of morning, they saw Jesus waiting for them by the lakeside, with breakfast ready cooked.

After they had eaten, Jesus walked along the shore with Peter. Three times over he asked Peter, 'Do you love me?'

Three times Peter had denied Jesus, but now three times he was able to tell Jesus that he loved him and wanted to be true to him.

'You know everything,' Peter said at last. 'You know that I love you.'

'Take care of my sheep and lambs,' Jesus told him. 'Follow me.'

Jesus was trusting Peter to look after his followers. Peter knew that, as well as teaching them, he must show them the kind of love and understanding that Jesus had shown to him. He would begin again.

Millions of others, since Peter's day, have found forgiveness through Jesus, and the strength to begin a new kind of life.

'NOW I AM A NEW MAN'

Vasili Ivanovich Kozlov was one of five children born into a poor peasant family in the Tartar Republic of the USSR. When he was only nine his father died, and the family was so poor that Kozlov was driven to stealing on the streets. He was only fifteen when he was first sent to prison. That was the beginning of a life of crime.

At last Kozlov was in despair. He wished that he could die — or live a completely different kind of life. He began to notice some

> Now the green blade riseth from the buried grain,
> Wheat that in dark earth many days has lain;
> Love lives again, that with the dead has been;
> Love is come again,
> Like wheat that springeth green.
>
> In the grave they laid him, Love whom men had slain,
> Thinking that never he would wake again,
> Laid in the earth like grain that sleeps unseen:
> Love is come again,
> Like wheat that springeth green. . .
>
> When our hearts are wintry, grieving, or in pain,
> Thy touch can call us back to life again,
> Fields of our hearts that dead and bare have been:
> Love is come again,
> Like wheat that springeth green.
>
> J. M. CRUM

prisoners who were different. They were in prison because they were Christians and, although that was their only crime, they did not curse or threaten, nor did they give up in despair and slash their wrists. They were gentle, brave and kind.

Before he was released, Kozlov had discovered the secret of their way of life and had become a Christian too. Before long he was in trouble with the authorities again — this time not for committing more crimes but for being a Christian.

At his trial, the judge read out his previous criminal record.

'It's true that I was once a thief and a criminal,' Kozlov answered. 'I deserved the sentences I received. But now my past is dead. The power of the blood of Christ has cleansed my wicked heart. Kozlov the criminal and gangster died a long time ago and was buried, while today, by the grace of God, Kozlov the Christian lives.'

EASTER WITH THE AUCA INDIANS

Easter 1976 was a specially joyful occasion for the Auca Indians. They held in their hands, for the first time, copies of St Mark's Gospel in their own language.

Don Johnson, from Wycliffe Bible Translators, who had flow in to the jungle air-strip with the precious Gospels, met with them on Easter Day in the thatched-roof shelter which was their church.

Kimo, headman of the church, prayed: 'Father God, you are alive. This is your day and all of us are here to worship you. You are all-powerful and all-knowing, Father God, your carving (the Auca word for Bible) is enough for everybody. We happily take it and having taken it, all of us read it and seeing it we say, "This is truth" . . . God, while we live in this land, your carving we will always obey.'

Don Johnson's thoughts went back to another day, ten years before, when he had been part of a small search party sent out to find five Wycliffe Bible Translators who had gone into Auca territory to make friends with the Auca Indians and tell them the Good News about Jesus. They found instead the murdered bodies of their comrades. But the relatives and friends of the martyred men were determined to go on bringing God's love to the Auca tribe.

Kimo, who had been one of the killers, found peace and forgiveness himself through the Easter message. Now the Aucas were planning a visit down river to an enemy tribe, not to wage war but to share with them God's love and forgiveness in Jesus.

It cost lives to bring the good news about Jesus to the Auca Indians: now they in turn risk death to pass on the message of God's love.

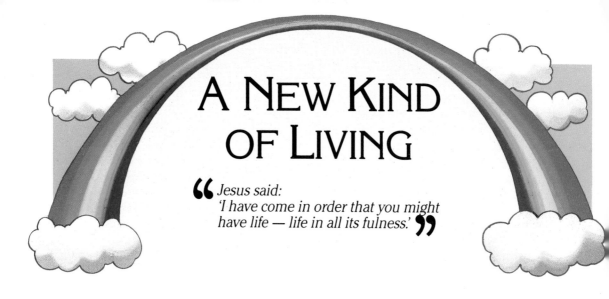

A NEW KIND OF LIVING

❝ *Jesus said:
'I have come in order that you might
have life — life in all its fulness.'* **❞**

ADVENTURE OVERSEAS

Squadron Leader Michael Cole is a Physical Education Officer with the RAF. He has enjoyed plenty of adventures from the days when he was a Boy Scout, and all through his Service career. But Mike now takes part in adventures that bring, not only thrills and spills to him and his teams, but much-needed help to people all over the world. Mike has run errands of mercy in a big way and, like a gentle giant, has transported a water-drilling rig to Ethiopia, an X-ray unit to Java and dinghies to Hongkong — with the help of numerous types of aircraft, and in the teeth of numberless delays because of government red tape.

Mike Cole hit the headlines with his River Rover hovercraft expeditions. The Christian life is always an adventure, though it is usually less dramatic than this.

More recently, Mike has been involved in his most daring and exciting achievements yet. Some of the world's great rivers provide splendid ready-made lines of communication — yet they cannot be used. No boat is capable of navigating the turbulent, swirling rapids which mark the rivers' course. In Nepal and Peru, for example, the inhabitants are forced to trek vast distances overland through dangerous terrain in order to get medical help, instead of travelling the short distance by river.

A medical missionary in Nepal recognized that a hovercraft, suitably adapted, might be able to overcome the problem by hovering over the surface of the rapids. He sent an SOS for help.

Mike took up the challenge, with God's help. He undertook the necessary fund-raising, supervised the building of the hovercraft and masterminded the production of what came to be called the River Rover. Then he led two expeditions, the first to Nepal and the next to the Amazonian jungle of Peru.

In Peru, the team achieved all their objectives. For three months they confronted the violence of the river, with its rapids, whirlpools and boulder-strewn banks. They took the hovercraft through the giant *barrial* rapids in the narrow headwaters of the Amazon, on a 1000 kilometre journey through some of the wildest parts of Amazonia. River Rover performed admirably.

The doctors and dentists in the team set up medical programmes in the riverside clinics which are manned by local medical assistants. Engineers installed radios, so that the base could be alerted in an emergency and the hovercraft called out. Other members of the team installed clean water supplies in three of the villages. Then the team trained local Peruvians to drive and maintain the hovercraft, which will remain in permanent service.

Not every member of the team shared Mike's Christian faith or agreed when, sometimes in the face of commonsense and Service training, he persisted on a course in order to follow what he believed to be God's way. But, as he told them one night, 'Once you have humbly told God that you have set no limits to what you are prepared to do, or where you are prepared to go, then, in the crisis, he will give you strength.'

ADVENTURE AT HOME

One morning, Ralph Capenerhurst decided he had had enough. For thirty-three years he had gone, regularly as clockwork, to his job on the shop floor of a Nottingham factory. He had served as a shop steward, been leader at his local church, and lived happily with his wife, Pat, bringing up their two daughters.

Now the family was off their hands and as Ralph looked ahead he could see nothing but comfortable retirement and a secure old age. And he didn't like what he saw. He thought of Bible heroes like Abraham, who had gone into unknown adventures with God when they were middle-aged and older.

A few days later he gave in his notice to a very surprised boss, and said goodbye to his safe pension.

The adventures that followed have not all been fun and Pat and Ralph admit that they have made mistakes. But they are sure that God was with them in every new crisis, turning it into something valuable for them and for other people too.

For a time Ralph experienced the pain and despair of being unemployed. Then, at fifty-five, he had the chance to train to be a minister in the Church of England.

Now, a few years later, he is back on the factory floors of Nottingham, this time as an industrial chaplain.

'My tools are my tongue and my ears,' Ralph says.

Because he understands how it feels to be trapped in a dead-end job, or to face unemployment, men talk to him and listen to him too. People who would never go near a church, pour out their fears, grievances and questions.

Ralph does not preach at them or talk theology. Like Jesus, he comes alongside and shows by his patience, humour and concern that Jesus is alive and cares for ordinary people.

New Beginnings

❝ *This is the end —*
for me the beginning of life **❞**
DIETRICH BONHOEFFER, just before his execution

Jesus promised his disciples: 'Because I live, you also will live!' Paul wrote: 'Christ has been raised from death as the guarantee that those who sleep in death will also be raised.'

ARCHBISHOP LUWUM

Janani Luwum was Archbishop of Uganda during President Amin's reign of terror. When Ugandan radio announced his death in a car accident in February 1977 many suspected foul play.

Sure enough, when the coffin was secretly opened, his face was found to be riddled with bullet wounds. Later it was alleged that Amin himself shot the archbishop during a final stormy interview.

The government cancelled plans for his burial at the cathedral at the eleventh hour and even forbade the holding of a memorial service there. But

From a tiny seed buried deep in the earth comes new life.

MR STAND-FAST
by John Bunyan

In the dream John Bunyan records in The Pilgrim's Progress *he sees one of the pilgrims, called Mr Stand-fast, receive a summons from his Master, to 'prepare for a change of life'. Soon, he must face the dark river of death . . .*

'This River hath been a terror to many, yea the thoughts of it also have often frighted me. But now methinks I stand easy . . . The waters indeed are to the palate bitter, and to the stomach cold; yet the thoughts of what I am going to, and of the conduct that waits for me on the other side, doth lie as a glowing coal at my heart.

'I see myself now at the end of my journey, my toilsome days are ended. I am going now to see that head that was crowned with thorns, and that face that was spit upon, for me.

'I have formerly lived by hear-say and faith, but now I go where I shall live by sight, and shall be with him, in whose company I delight myself.

'I have loved to hear my Lord spoken of, and wherever I have seen the print of his shoe in the earth, there I have coveted to set my foot too . . .'

Now while he was thus in discourse his countenance changed . . . and after he had said, 'Take me, for I come unto thee,' he ceased to be seen of them.

But glorious it was, to see how the open region was filled with horses and chariots, with trumpeters and pipers, with singers, and players on stringed instruments, to welcome the pilgrims as they went up and followed one another in at the beautiful Gate of the City.

---

hundreds defied the ban and flocked to the cathedral to demonstrate their loyalty to Christ and to the archbishop they had loved.

After the service they filed out of the church still singing, and gathered round the grave that had been prepared in vain. The retired, elderly archbishop spoke:

'When we see an empty grave,' he said, 'it reminds us of when the angels spoke to the women at the empty grave of Jesus at that first Easter.'

Then he cried out in a loud voice, 'He is not dead: he is risen!'

The crowd responded with joy. Because Jesus was alive, they knew that their beloved Janani Luwum was alive too.

DAVID WATSON

In February 1982, David Watson, a widely known preacher and writer, died of cancer. During his last illness he wrote a book, *Fear No Evil*, describing his feelings and beliefs about death:

'In one sense,' he wrote, 'the Christian is not preparing for death. Essentially he is preparing for *life*, abundant life in all its fulness . . . The best and purest joys on earth are only a shadow of the reality that God has prepared for us in Christ. Eternal life begins as soon as we receive Christ as our Saviour . . . When I die, it is my firm conviction that I shall be more alive than ever . . . The actual moment of dying is still shrouded in mystery, but as I keep my eyes on Jesus I am not afraid. Jesus has already been through death for us, and will be with us when we walk through it ourselves.'

THE CELEBRATION THAT GOES ON FOR EVER

Our book began where Easter begins, in the long, lean days of Lent, which end in the black despair of Good Friday. But with Easter Day come life, light and joy. Jesus' death was not the end, nor was it the terrible mistake that it had seemed at first to be. Jesus came to earth to give his life, in order to make peace between God and us and to bring the whole universe back to God. His rising to life proved that he had won the battle against wickedness, darkness and death, once for all.

All these events happened nearly 2,000 years ago, and it often seems that evil and suffering and violence still rule the world. But Jesus made two promises which make the final victory of good and justice certain.

Before he left the world to go back to God his Father, Jesus promised to send his Holy Spirit to live within his followers, bringing them courage and strength to defeat wrong and fear in their own lives. Peter and his friends were changed people when the Holy Spirit came to them on the first Whit Sunday. And God the Holy Spirit still comes to those who have found new life in Jesus, transforming their lives.

Jesus also promised that he himself would return to our world one day. The hope of his coming-again excited and thrilled the early church and it has encouraged and cheered Christians of every century since.

The Bible says that Jesus will come, not as an unknown carpenter and preacher, but as the King over all kings and the ruler of the universe. He will drive away greed and violence and selfishness and bring in a world of peace and love for all who are his subjects.

Then, at last, it will be true that 'the kingdom of the world has become the kingdom of our Lord and of his Christ, and he shall reign for ever and ever'.

So the celebration that began at Easter will never end.

Christ Jesus lay in death's strong bands
For our offences given;
But now at God's right hand he stands
And brings us life from heaven:
Wherefore let us joyful be,
And sing to God right thankfully
Loud songs of Hallelujah!
Hallelujah!

It was a strange and dreadful strife,
When life and death contended;
The victory remained with life,
The reign of death was ended:
Stript of power, no more he reigns:
An empty power alone remains;
His sting is lost for ever.
Hallelujah!

So let us keep the festival
Whereto the Lord invites us;
Christ is himself the joy of all,
The Sun that warms and lights to us;
By his grace he doth impart
Eternal sunshine to the heart;
The night of sin is ended.
Hallelujah!

MARTIN LUTHER, 1483-1546

INDEX